The SUNDAY EXPRESS Book of
EUROPEAN HOLIDAYS

The
SUNDAY EXPRESS
Book of
EUROPEAN
HOLIDAYS

Lewis De Fries

Illustrations by Bill Martin

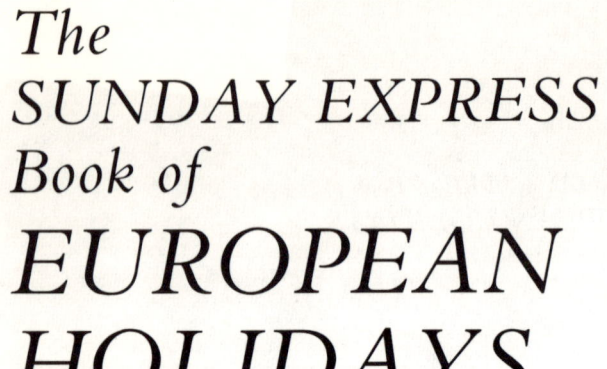

A Robin Clark/*Sunday Express* Publication

First published by Robin Clark Ltd.
in association with the *Sunday Express*, 1984

Robin Clark Ltd.
A member of the Namara Group
27/29 Goodge Street, London WiP iFD

British Library Cataloguing in Publication Data

The Sunday Express book of European holidays.
    1. Europe—Description and travel—1971–
    I. De Fries, Lewis
    914'.0455   D923

    ISBN 0-86072-076-4

Typeset by MC Typeset, Chatham, Kent
Printed and bound in Great Britain
By Mackays of Chatham Ltd, Kent

CONTENTS

INTRODUCTION

Chance made me specialize in travel. It all began in the unlikely, windswept setting of Heligoland, the tiny German island in the North Sea. As a general features journalist I'd been sent by the *Sunday Express* to report on a little-known historical link: in Victorian days Heligoland was British.

Someone had told us a strange story of how a group of very elderly survivors of British rule hid Union Jacks in their cellars from the Gestapo and remained loyal to the old country. We were certainly not planning to recommend the place to tourists, but I could not avoid referring to the fact that the Germans had transformed the island from blitzed desolation into a tourist attraction, complete with hotels and other holiday facilities.

Not that the hotel where I stayed was exactly bursting with goodwill and hospitality – on my last day checking out, formalities were conducted in my absence and without my knowledge with Teutonic efficiency. I returned to find my bags ready packed and awaiting me on the doorstep. It seemed I had unwittingly exceeded the check-out time; the room was wanted for someone else.

I suppose I should not have been surprised. After all, Queen Victoria had been dead a long time, we had blasted the place during the Second World War and when Germany surrendered in 1945 we repaid the loyalty of the old people there by forcibly evacuating the entire population and turning Heligoland into a firing range to use up our surplus bombs and shells.

The BBC had also developed over the years the habit of blaming Heligoland as the place of origin for any bad weather that happened to hit the British Isles. So there was no longer any reason to love us; I was baffled by the locals who insisted that they did.

However, what I wrote about Heligoland some twenty years ago turned out to be more of what newspapers call a 'puff' for tourism than a straightforward news feature – in some way the idea of the sheer novelty of a Briton holidaying there broke through. And it more or less set the pattern for me as a travel writer – a career for which I might have been regarded as being singularly ill-equipped. I hadn't travelled much and my school-days were hardly distinguished by any talent for foreign languages.

I had not even inherited a bump of direction. My father, a lifelong Londoner, was hopeless at finding his way about and when appealed to for directions to any part of the metropolis invariably recommended a No. 20 bus – a route non-existent at the time. I can't imagine his reaction, had he been alive, to my spending about ten months of every twelve touring the world on behalf of readers of the *Sunday Express*. Probably he would have shared my mother's dismay at the very idea. Until the day she died she regarded anywhere more than three miles out of Dover as a mysterious dark semi-civilized world where it was fatal for any Briton to drink the water and swarthy villains were lurking around every corner with stilettos poised.

Nor, I am sure, did she believe that I actually ate and enjoyed the strange-sounding foreign food I described. Which brings me to the touching concern so many readers have about the penalty they are convinced I pay for all this eating and drinking. One wrote saying he was sure I was a cross between Orson Welles, Charles Laughton and Billy Bunter. I was never sylph-like, but I refute such suggestions with indignation. I burn up a lot of energy in this job, I tell them, because I'm always on the move. 'Lucky devil,' they write. 'Living off the fat of the land and basking in sunshine and all those hotels. Always on holiday.'

Now I don't expect sympathy and I'll readily admit that I would hate a nine-to-five job; but the truth is that travel writing has as much routine, hard work and frustrations attached to it as any other branch of journalism – or any other profession. After all, who seriously believes that a travel agent is always swanning about enjoying himself or a chef is always gorging away in the kitchen?

I look upon my work as constructive reporting: I'd been a reporter and feature writer for many years before specializing in travel. You go, you experience, you observe and you write about it as you see it and you don't consult the clock for knocking-off time. Of course eating is a pleasant aspect of the work, but this, without any pretensions on my part to being a gourmet, is an essential part of one's services to readers. Food is a vital holiday ingredient and especially when the weather is not at its best and you are not going to miss the sunshine or a romantic moonlit evening by lingering over your lunch or dinner. Spending longer at table also helps to dispel the conviction of some Frenchmen that we are a nation of moronic fast eaters concerned only with filling a hole in our stomachs.

I also try to put over the delights of eating in local style. There's no point in using your space to write about food of the sort you can have without leaving Britain – or even your own dining table. So if I dwell on the pleasures of eating lovingly prepared seafood, game in wine and cream sauce and soufflé glacé Grand Marnier rather than the soup, steak and chips and creme caramel so many French families seem to choose when they visit a restaurant, it is for a good reason. I would not be doing my job properly if I failed to show that the traditional image of France as a gastronomic paradise of discriminating people is being maintained even in these days of faddish, inadequate and highly pricey *nouvelle cuisine*.

You'll notice, too, that France has the largest share of any single country in my selection of European holidays. I make no apology for that. France to me is still the tourist country par excellence, still has what the average Briton regards as the most 'continental' atmosphere of all.

I recall a reader who once asked me where he could go to find this special atmosphere on his first trip abroad and I recommended France. A few weeks later he wrote again, thanking me profusely, saying he had crossed the Channel, found a British-run boarding house in Calais, had English breakfast and full Sunday lunch, could see the White Cliffs of Dover in the distance and after a week was so foreign-orientated that he had to spend an equal time in Norfolk to pull himself together before returning to work.

On an occasion like that you're tempted to write back recommending Boulogne for the following year's adventure. But on reflection you don't do any such thing – the success of each holiday depends on how easily each individual is satisfied. To suggest that they don't know what they are missing by not going further into the mysterious wilds of abroad strikes me as merely patronizing.

France also has captured the leading share of the ever increasing tendency towards individual holidays, with or without a car. And it is ideal for every type of vacation I am featuring in this selection: the short Channel hop out of season, the city weekend, the leisurely motoring holiday with stays in pleasant little family-run country hotels or camp sites as well as the 'orthodox' fortnight by the sea, packaged or not according to your preference.

Think of its rich variety: the romantic stillness of the Vendee's reed-bordered waterways, the superb mountain scenery of the Jura and the majesty of Mont Blanc and Savoie, the velvet green slopes of Gascony and the Mediterranean charm of Provence as well as the stylishness of the Cote d'Azur, the rugged salty air of Brittany and Normandy so close to home, the timeless lure of Paris. And of course the marvellous food . . .

Never in France have I undergone mindblowing conversations while tracing a local speciality, although the situation certainly applies to a number of other countries:

'What is your real local dish?'

'We call it a plomph – there is no word for it in English.'

'How do you eat it?'

'With a knife and fork.'

'No – I don't mean that. Is it a starter, a main dish or a dessert?'

'It is a plomph – it is a meal in itself.'

'Can you tell me where to find it?'

'At this time of year – impossible.'

'When did you have it last yourself?'

'When my grandmother made it – she died twenty-five years ago.'

'But can it be found sometimes in some restaurants?'

'No – only in private houses.'

'So a tourist will not see it?'

'No.'

We travel writers work hard on your behalf, we really do. What you read in the paper represents just the tip of the iceberg.

France to me somehow encapsulates Europe – and of all the continents Europe is my favourite, my first love. I sampled France first of all – it was my European foretaste, but I soon learnt in the best of all ways that there is more to Europe than France. Italy has so much to offer, too. What more glorious contrast can there be than between the romantic Alpine atmosphere of the Italian Tyrol in the far north and the lazy, so Italianate world of the Neapolitan Riviera and Capri and sweeping as far south as you can get, the sheer magic of Calabria?

Contrast isn't everything of course – but even a cosy little country like Holland, so easily covered in a few hours, has different faces to show the visitor: the sophistication of cosmopolitan Amsterdam, the style and grace of The Hague and the windmills and grassy dykes of simple Zeeland.

But the richest contrasts of all are to be found within the boundaries of Europe as a whole and I have tried to represent them in this selection of articles of mine which have appeared in the *Sunday Express* in recent years. For Europe just has everything; it is a holiday world in itself: beaches, gorgeous landscapes, mountains, lakes, handsome, treasure-filled cities, crisp northern air and Mediterranean warmth and colour. As Britons we've every right to feel at home there – for who discovered them for tourism if not us? In days when Africa and America were as remote to tourism as the moon, we were making the Europeans conscious of what they had to offer.

I have updated prices where necessary, but reading the facts as I have given them you must also take into account that tourism is an ever-changing scene. Restaurants I have named may have either changed hands, or even gone out of business altogether. You find different conditions prevailing on almost each successive visit to a country or region and you must also bear in mind seasonal variations of cost of produce, fluctuating exchange rate and so on.

Look on this selection as a mere taste, a tantalizing taste, I hope, of what richness, both of nature and of man-made beauty, Europe represents. I've chosen carefully among my favourite regions and looking through my files has revived so many memories that the final selection has been hard going, for I have had for reasons of space to discard so much. Going back through the years I stand again on the headlands, beside the lovely lakes deep in volcanic craters and among the matchless wild hydrangeas of the rugged little Azores – halfway to America but still within the bounds of Europe, the group of tiny Portuguese islands far out in the Atlantic I have had a love affair with for years.

I have watched again the mighty sea-eagle sweep down to its prey in the chilly waters of Norway's Far North. I drive once more through the misty landscape of an old Dutch master. I climb the Eiffel Tower for that glorious view across the Seine. I feel my blood tingle to the sensuous pipes and drums accompanying a bellydancer in the smoky, colourful atmosphere of a nightclub high in an ancient tower soaring among the minarets of Istanbul. I remember the fabulous sunsets over Vesuvius and the Bay of Naples, the lushness of Capri. My footsteps echo once again through the treasure halls of Florence. I see the islands, the dazzling white cottages, the temples, mountains and the superb colours of Greece. I want to search anew for the windmill Don Quixote charged with levelled lance, catch again the first glimpse of the Alhambra springing over the Andalusian horizon like a glittering image, and long for the sight and sound of Spanish beauties dancing flamenco to the swelling strains of 'Granada'.

I remember the sheer joy of discovering Dutch ice cream and spicy apple cake, the richness of a Swiss chocolate gateau, the akevitt that seemed to explode in my mouth but gave me a marvellous appetite for a Norwegian cold table. I can scent the fragrant steam wreathing around the little kitchens of countless French seaside and country restaurants and the beaming face of Madame when you tell her the food is fantastic. I relive the bliss of the best sizzling paella I have ever eaten, the scent of roasting chestnuts on the Spanish Steps of winter in Rome and find myself craving for just one whiff of the mimosa which sweetens the uplands of the Cote d'Azur and the tang of pine and eucalyptus.

My job has been to travel extensively on a purely professional basis, to see Europe in an objective fashion and to present it as a guide for the pleasure of others. I would like to think that my own personal delight in so much I have seen and experienced, somehow comes through. I have so often started for home thinking wistfully that my stay was not long enough and feeling positively envious of those who will follow in my footsteps with so much more time to spare. Of course I have tastes of my own; there are spots I like more than others, and probably the hardest aspect of travel writing is to try to project yourself into the minds of your readers and see Europe as they do.

At the same time, a travel writer does have the luxury of putting his own personal views – everything he writes he must believe in, must be prepared to stand by, even if he has the advantage of being able to make a wider comparison than most.

I often get letters from readers who ask plaintively: 'Don't you ever have a rainy day, stay in a disappointing hotel, have a rotten meal?' Of course I do, but I've yet to pick a spot where all the food is lousy, the hotels are uncomfortable and the weather constantly atrocious. If all these vital factors were against it, the place would neither have become a tourist attraction from the start nor would I see any point in describing it.

It would be rewarding to think that the thousands of *Sunday Express* readers who have gone on the journeys I have taken have found the same delights and shared my pleasure; but it would be sheer arrogance on my part to believe they have always agreed with every word I have written. So much depends on personal taste. I have had many of what diplomats describe as frank exchanges of ideas with readers, but I'm happy to say that most of the hundreds of letters I receive back my views.

As I said earlier, this book is a mere taste of what is in store for you on the broad face of Europe – it is not a detailed guide, but, confined to the narrow space of newspaper travel pages, just a rough indication of what to expect.

Many of the places I have chosen will be familiar to you; others will be virgin territory so far as you are concerned. I shall both envy those seeing my favourites for the first time and feel glad I have revived memories of past trips for readers who may be inspired by reading this book to go again and see Europe with fresh eyes.

For however familiar a holiday destination, however well you think you know a region or a city there is always some pleasure, some aspect, some refinement you missed the first time. I should know . . .

Finally, although I have included in this book as many of my favourite holiday places as space permits, I come to the question people like me are asked repeatedly: Where do I spend my *own* holidays? The answer is a tiny idyllic valley, the domain of foxes, owls, deer and the occasional badger. From the top of the slope overlooking it I can bask in a glorious 300-degree panorama of Surrey and Sussex at their best. Deep in the valley is a little Tudor cottage with the most comfortable bed and complete with my favourite of all cooks.

I haven't any intention of telling you how to get there.

FRANCE

1 BERRY – THE HEARTLAND

Sancerre was waiting for me high on its little hill, its stone houses a rich cream beneath dark red roofs gleaming in the late afternoon sun. The setting was idyllic: the town surrounded by the vineyards which produced the fine wine bearing its name, the wooded slopes beyond blue in the haze and the loveliest river in all France, the Loire, moving lazily in the distance.

This was the perfect place to relax after my drive from a busy motorway into a peaceful little domain in the very heart of the country.

Winding roads had taken me past reed-fringed lakes where herons and cranes watched me solemnly through rustling oak forests where deer flitted across rolling meadows dotted with ancient farmhouses.

Pinnacled châteaux and majestic old fortresses rose above the trees, peacocks displayed their bright plumage beside ancient moats where swans glided. This was country France at her incomparable best.

That night as the moon rose over Sancerre I drove from my hotel down the hill towards the Loire. But I had no plan to cross the bridge into Burgundy. There was no better way to end my first day in Berry than to dine in local style beside the open fireplace in a softly-lit restaurant fragrant with early spring flowers.

That restaurant in Sancerre's riverside suburb of St Thibault did not offer *haute cuisine*, but delicious French country cooking.

First, I had full flavoured terrine of wild boar from the forests where ancient kings and nobles hunted. It was garnished with cherries, olives and tiny pickles and served with salad. Then came a *vol au vent* filled with cream and mushrooms.

For my main course I had baby chicken with onions in a sauce of Sancerre wine. The creamiest goat cheese you can find anywhere in France was followed by the best of all Berry desserts – apple *tarte tatin* rich in caramel. And the price with coffee and a pichet of wine was just £7.80.

That night I was about as deep in France as it is possible to be. On my drive to Sancerre that day I had gone over a village crossroads where the tricolor fluttered above an ancient stone column marking the country's exact centre.

Yet for all the fame of Sancerre wine the Berry countryside is still unknown to so many thousands of British visitors who love France.

For what was once the oldest French ducal domain of all – the title of Duke of Berry was held only by princes of royal blood – is just slightly too far south of the Loire valley and too far east of the favourite routes south from the Channel ports to be automatically part of most Britons' motoring holiday plans.

The locals will tell you wryly that the last time we came in any numbers was in the Middle Ages when we raided across the River Creuse from what were then the French lands of the English kings. Today the great castles built by each nation to protect their frontier still stand near the Creuse banks.

Today too, the old ducal lands are two French *départements* named after other rivers which flow through them – Indre and Cher – and though they offer so much delight to anyone with a passion for France, most Britons just don't know what they are missing.

There is that gorgeous countryside for one thing. There are châteaux to visit which are every bit as majestic as the more famous royal châteaux in the Loire valley and, unlike these, many have the added advantage of being so much more than cold museums packed with treasures.

Many of the ancient families whose crest they bear still live there and a few even offer bed and breakfast. Spring seems to come early and summer lingers on. So there is a pleasantly long period of the year when it is warm enough to get a tan, to picnic deep in the old hunting forests, to swim, sail, water-ski, canoe, ride or play tennis.

And there are waters rich in trout, carp, pike and perch.

If you want sophisticated nightlife don't go within a hundred miles of Berry. Apart from a discotheque or two and a few little bars and cafes Berry is as far removed from nightlife as it is from mass tourism and package tours. For a French country holiday for a family with a car Berry is perfection.

Where to stay? You've the choice of a town or country setting. Berry's capital, Bourges, has a cobbled old quarter lined by timber-framed houses and is full of charm.

Aubigny is a quieter smaller version of it. On the River Creuse there is Argenton, one of the prettiest towns in all France where balconied houses lean out over the water to resemble a backdrop for a medieval pageant.

There is idyllic La Chatre and stately Issoudun, dominated by a tower where Richard the Lion Heart was wounded in a long-forgotten siege. I also liked St Amand Montrond where green hills sweep down to the edge of town.

And if, like me, you think there is no country setting quite so French as that of the Loire, you will make for Sancerre and St Thibault.

A small hotel offering half board costs from about £5 a day and there are camp sites where a family of four with cars and tent pay from £4 in daily fees. But an ever-increasing number of visitors prefer to stay deep in the countryside in furnished farm cottages which can be rented from about £70 a week buying their chickens, fruit and vegetables direct from the farmer.

If you prefer a package deal, one of the ferry companies operating a cross-Channel service charges £51 for each of four people, including their car, for two weeks' stay in a cottage.

The humblest village takes pride in a small restaurant guaranteed to delight anyone with a taste for French country cooking.

I remember a cheerful little inn at drowsy Plampied where for just over £8 I dined superbly beginning with a typical local speciality – onion tarts served with a bowl of cream. You remove the pastry lid and add the cream to your taste.

The main course was salmon from the Loire grilled to perfection and garnished with mushrooms, fresh lemon and anchovie butter.

Dessert was a delicious ice cream gateau topped with raspberries and whipped cream and the price included coffee and a half-litre of wine.

Wherever you choose to stay, the attractions of the region are all within easy reach by car on quiet roads – Berry is about ninety miles from east to west and 120 from north to south. In minutes you could drive from a simple lunch at a little inn or a picnic spot in a peaceful glade to the majesty of a great château set in its own park.

And however turbulent their history might have been, those great buildings add so much to the peace and romance of Berry today. I remember the stillness of Valencay, a stillness so complete that I could almost hear the pen of Talleyrand, Napoleon's wily foreign minister whose home it was, scratching away as he turned his master's grandiose schemes into diplomatic realities.

The sun shone through the great windows to light up the table from Vienna on which the victorious allies redrew the map of Europe after Napoleon's fall.

On the lawns outside, peacocks displayed their glowing colours and birds sang in the great trees in the park. And standing there I thought how easy it was for a completely relaxed visitor, even on a brief stay, to fall in love with the atmosphere of Berry.

Sadly, Talleyrand in his crowded, scheming life was probably too preoccupied to notice.

Dinner in Saint-Thibault – Restaurant l'Auberge.
Lunch at Plampied – Restaurant Aux Marais.

2 THE MIDI – PYRENEES

The early mist of a Pyrenean summer day drifted gently around me as I drove out of town.

I could not resist looking back – already the three lofty towers of Foix Castle were in sunshine.

Yes, it was going to be the perfect morning with the sun soon returning to the narrow streets below the castle walls and sparkling on the River Ariege.

Ahead of me, now clear in the morning light, were the snow-capped Pyrenees rising to 10,000 feet and dividing this fascinating little holiday region of south-west France from Spain and Andorra.

The previous day I had thought that nothing could quite match the satisfaction of turning off the busy roads south to find myself in the tranquil atmosphere of a *département* thousands of British tourists miss and even the French from other regions barely know. I could not have been more wrong.

For the further I drove on the winding roads into the mountains the more I was delighted with what I saw.

Lush valleys lay far below me, ancient castles stood on the heights, villages of stone cottages, their balconies bright with roses, echoed to the sound of cow bells and sheep fleeces hung drying outside cottage doors.

Rivers more dramatic than the Ariege – it has given its name to the holiday land I had chosen – creamed and splashed over dozens of tiny falls as perfect for canoe enthusiasts as the pine-fringed lakes were for trout fishermen.

Sunlight dappled huge forests of beech and birch.

I looked into Spain but I had no plans across the frontier from France. Ariege is small enough – a mere forty miles from north to south and roughly the same from west to east, but it has everything a lover of a French country holiday could desire.

The air was warmer in the valleys as I drove down hungry for

my lunch. The little town of Le Mas d'Azil was filled with
market-day bustle.

But beyond the plane trees bordering the main square I
spotted the banks of roses and the bright sunshades of a
restaurant terrace. And soon I was being served with food as fine
as the scenery.

First came full-flavoured charcuterie, then venison in red wine
and garnished with tiny forest mushrooms and roasted potatoes.

There was a selection of mountain cheeses and for dessert I
chose ice cream topped with armagnac-laced whipped cream
and served with plums in real local style. And the cost with
coffee and wine was £6.50.

You don't go to Ariege for sophisticated entertainment
although it boasts a solitary casino at a swish spa called
Ax-les-Thermes in the far south-east.

Nightlife generally is simple enough – a handful of discotheques and little bars and cafes. But nightlife is far from your mind
when you get the first view of its scenery.

To help you enjoy the place even more, you can play tennis,
ride horses, swim, go boating on those fast-flowing mountain
rivers and fish in the peaceful lakes. You can take a boat trip
along a mysterious underground river. And there are many old
towns and castles to explore.

Towns like Mirepoix, where you drive through an ancient
gateway to find yourself behind the towering walls of a city the
twentieth century has barely penetrated. In the main square the
roses dazzle you and the timber-framed houses stand on huge
wooden stilts forming a colonnade through which you walk.

And as if there are not enough treasures around you can try
for some of your own to take home. In the river near the village
of Caumont you can even pan for gold. It costs you just over
£100 for a five-day course. All you need is a pair of gumboots
and a lot of patience.

Weatherbeaten types who look like relics of the Californian
gold rush supply expertise and traditional equipment – sieves,
shovels, pans, and one concession to the twentieth century: an
electric pump to sort out the stuff you bring from the river bed.

You are unlikely to get your money back. A few glittering

In the foothills of the Pyrenees . . .
the town of Foix nestles alongside the River Ariege

grains worth about £5 constitute the average haul for your stay, but the experience is worth it.

Some people may consider it foolish to spend £100 just for the chance to get a few glittering grains worth about £5. But others will think it money well spent, and working there in the Ariege sun – the high summer temperature soars into the eighties – will do wonders both for your thirst and your tan.

There are one or two package tours to the region from Britain but this is a country above all for the independent traveller with a car.

And to my mind there isn't a better way of enjoying it than to rent a family-sized cottage from around £70 a week and buy your food direct from the farmers or from the village shops and treat yourself to some meals in small restaurants which charge

around £5 for three courses with wine and coffee. If you prefer
to camp, daily fees can cost a family as little as £3. There are also
small hotels charging from around £10 a day half board.

Le Mas d'Azil, Saint Girons, Tarascon on the Ariege below
Foix and Foix itself are all pleasant towns in which to stay.

But for smaller, quieter places there is nothing to beat little
Castillon and Sentein in the west of the region. Close to them is
the lovely lake of Bethmale and the start of the area's most
breathtaking scenic road, the Route des Grandes Pyrenees and
the romantic splendours of the Biros Valley.

But however deeply you fall in love with the countryside –
whether you go in summer when the valleys are blue with
gentians, or in autumn, when the colours are incomparable –
give yourself a day to visit Toulouse, capital of the Midi
Pyrenees and France's fourth city.

Fountains play in its leafy squares, the tree-lined canals and
sweeping bridges give it a Parisian air. Everywhere graceful old
buildings have rose-pink facades which gleam in the sun.

And the restaurants are fabulous. I can happily recommend an
elegant place near Saint Etienne cathedral, where, for £8, I was
served the lightest of cheese soufflés, followed by duck in a
cream and sorrel sauce with sauté potatoes, and then a dessert of
pancake filled with bananas and blueberries and topped with
mocha parfait and whipped cream. And the price included coffee
and a half-litre of wine.

But even deep in the countryside you can find a touch of *haute
cuisine* in the most unexpected places. At the end of a narrow
rough road, little more than a farm track near Pamiers, a few
miles north of Foix, I dined on my last night in the region and
although, at £11, it was easily the most expensive meal of my
entire trip, I could not have been better pleased.

I ate in an old farmhouse, now a charming auberge.
Candlelight flickered on old beams.

I tucked into trout prepared to perfection with walnut
stuffing. Then there was my main course of goose.

That goose was a masterpiece – with it came a delicious sauce
of brandy, peppers, shallots and cream and a generous helping of
mushrooms.

For dessert there was a coupe made with some of the best strawberries I have eaten anywhere. The half-bottle of wine was just right and the coffee could not have been bettered in Paris.

The fire died down, the candlelight seemed to become more mellow. As mellow as my own mood as I lingered over my coffee and savoured the memory of that meal.

Outside the moon silvered the Pyrenean meadows. And I felt sorrier than ever that next morning I would have to take the road home.

Lunch in Toulouse – La Mareschale.
Lunch at Le Mas d'Azil – Hotel Gardel.
Meal in inn – Le Relais de Baulias, near Escosse.

3 FINISTERE –
SALTY BRITTANY

It was perfection – the spring day filled with sunshine and the two worlds of Finistere to enjoy.

One was behind me now: the last of the gulls bobbed in the creamy wake of the motorboat as the swell subsided and the salty tang from the meeting place of the Atlantic and the Channel gave way to the sweetness of the pines on the river bank, with solemn herons and stately châteaux adding to the atmosphere of rural peace.

Two worlds – and here was the second to bask in on the River Odet leading deep into the heart of Finistere from the coast at Benodet to the towers of dreamy old Quimper.

I stepped ashore to walk cobbled streets lined with old gabled houses and under the trees and past the banks of dazzling camellias beside the river.

My £2.50 lunch in a creperie near the cathedral was typically Breton: two delicious pancakes – one filled with scrambled egg, ham and cheese, the other with hot chocolate, with a quarter-litre of refreshing cider to accompany them and coffee to end.

There was a lazy-paced return journey on the last leg of one of Brittany's most popular river excursions in mellow afternoon sunshine to the sea and the whirling gulls again. I was back on the coast in time to see the fishing boats returning with the day's catch and to admire the sunset from the lofty height of France's most powerful lighthouse on the romantic Pointe de Penmarch.

But my first full day in Finistere had one more delight to offer: dinner at my destination, Concarneau, close to the ramparts which make the lovely old Breton town a smaller cosier version of St Malo. I could have chosen a less expensive restaurant, but a perfect day demanded a perfect round-off – and dinner was just right for my mood of contentment.

The old fishing port at Concarneau

First they served me a huge platter of superb seafood – clams, langoustines, crab and four big oysters, complete with garnish of mayonnaise and fresh lemon.

My main course was bream cooked in white wine, cream, and mushrooms, accompanied by mixed vegetables and airy vol-au-vent-type pastry. My dessert, chosen with difficulty from a big tempting selection, was a masterly blackcurrant and raspberry charlotte – the best charlotte I have ever tasted.

With coffee and a half-bottle of wine I was charged £11, but I did not feel I was paying too much for the pleasure of the experience.

For all the fact that bustling, popular St Malo is as much a part of Brittany as Concarneau, it could have been a million miles away that evening. For Finistere, the westernmost tip of France, is a very special part of the Breton domain.

Here, where old ladies still wear traditional elaborate white head-dresses and so many of the locals still speak the old Breton tongue to the despair of French visitors from other regions, custom has defied the passing centuries.

And what a lovely underrated corner of France it is, with its pink headlands topped with pines, its 200 miles of smooth sands lining sweeping bays and looking out on two seas. And inland, there is a countryside with scenery ranging from green rolling hills laced with winding rivers to rustling forests and wild moors.

It is a land of folk legends; to me one of the most fascinating is that the more appealing southern half was once so admired by visiting Cornishmen that they not only settled there but gave it the name of their native land they thought it so resembled. Today southern Finistere is still called Cornouaille.

Today, too, admiring Britons still come to Finistere from our far west: on the fast comfortable ferries from Plymouth to the pleasant little northern Finistere resort of Roscoff. And some of those who make the sea journey from Portsmouth to St Malo are lured west to Finistere to see for themselves just how different it is from anywhere else in western France.

Finistere offers so much: a pleasant early spring filled with flowers and so often a fine summer and a long lingering autumn. The breakers might cream majestically beneath the benign gaze of the Virgin statue at France's Land's End, the Pointe du Raz, but the clear waters in the lovely sand-fringed bays nearby and in a score of peaceful little coves can be delightfully calm.

You go to Finistere to swim, sail, water-ski and windsurf, to fish for bass and mullet and to dive for crab, to ride, play golf, tennis, join excursions to ruggedly beautiful islands or head inland on boat trips up some of France's loveliest rivers.

You can catch salmon and trout, explore majestic castles and intriguing grottoes and enjoy the timeless atmosphere of attractive old towns and villages of sturdy granite where the British are by long custom the favourite overseas visitors.

It isn't the least expensive part of France: a comfortable hotel with half board won't cost less than around £11 a day for independent travellers. But package tours, including taking your car on the ferries from Portsmouth and Plymouth, are good value.

A nine-day holiday with hotel and breakfast costs from £109, a place in a seaside apartment for a week is £78, and if you prefer the country life you pay from just over £50 a head for a week in a farm cottage. There are also special packages for campers.

Where to stay? In the far south is romantic Pont Aven, the inspiration of artists for centuries. Here a waterwheel turns in the heart of a town of jumbled little houses, the Aven banks glow with flowers, and nearby at the lovely spot where the river broadens into its estuary to meet the sea between forested banks you can have bed and breakfast in a pinnacled château, relaxing in tapestried splendour but paying no more than you would in an hotel.

There's my own favourite, Concarneau, a few miles to the north-west of Pont Aven, and Benodet with its superb pine setting and its touch of sophistication – it has Finistere's only casino. Set in some of the most beautiful bays of all are Audierene, Douarnenez-Treboul, intimate little Pentrez with its fishing village atmosphere, romantic old Morgat and Ste Anne La Palud.

If you yearn for the simple rugged life, stay on Ushant, the island guarding the Channel entrance.

Don't look for sophisticated nightlife, apart from that casino at Benodet. But if after a day in the Finistere sun you're happy with a discotheque or two, some folk dancing and occasional visiting singers or a friendly little bar filled with the locals, then this very special corner of France is ideal.

Close to the sea but in a perfect country setting at Plogonnec I found an isolated farm auberge one evening which gave me the best country meal – all home-produced local food – of my Finistere trip. Under venerable beams lit with the flickering glow of a huge log fire, a group of sturdy old Breton farmers sat talking in their own special language.

Madame broke off to bustle to the kitchen to prepare my country feast – simple but delicious. First she gave me smoked trout served with sweetcorn and eggs in a piquant sauce. Then came tender pork in cream and wine with roast potatoes, followed by salad and creamy cheese.

For dessert there was a huge slice of feathery light blueberry pie. With coffee and a half-bottle of wine I paid £6.50.

As happy and replete, I headed for the door, the old men

raised their glasses to me in courteous farewell. My hostess peered out into the moonlight. 'A north wind,' she said. 'My friends tell me that tomorrow will be another good day.'

'Tell them,' I said – and I meant it – 'that every day is good in Finistere, even when it rains.'

There was a roar of approval – the old place positively shook. And the farmers toasted me again. Madame beamed. 'Monsieur,' she said, 'tonight you have made some friends for life.'

Meal at Concarneau – Relais La Coquille, Rue du Moros.
Farm dinner at Plogonnec – Auberge de Leurbiriou.

4 MAGIC OF THE JURA

The forecasters had been firm on the point – the weather was set fair for the Jura mountains.

But in the night a summer storm had broken the long, dry spell, and although everything was fresh and green and it was warm enough to breakfast on the terrace of my hotel in the hills above Besançon, a mist hung over the valley and to me the day did not look promising.

'Where's the famous view of Mont Blanc?' I grumbled to the waiter.

'Patience Monsieur,' he counselled. 'By the time you get to Mont d'Or the weather will be perfect. The mist is a good sign.'

I'm ashamed to say I drove down the valley unconvinced, despite the fact that after breakfast the mist seemed slightly less dense. I bought myself a typical Jura picnic in Besançon and climbed the high hill above the winding Doubs river to the ramparts of the lofty citadel to spy out the land.

No doubt now, things *were* improving. Gradually the panorama of wooded mountains, the jumbled roofs of the town, the river sweeping into the distance were coming clear.

Perhaps the waiter was right after all. Perhaps I *was* going to enjoy my lunch of paté, fresh country bread, a marvellous creamy Jura cheese, fruit and a bottle of wine on the wild lovely plateau of Mont d'Or, with Mont Blanc glittering on the horizon before me and the Swiss lake of Neuchatel gleaming in the sun far below.

No perhaps about it. At the end of the winding road through the fir forests of Mont d'Or the mist had vanished. And not only Mont Blanc but the huge range of other mighty Alpine peaks were in full glory on the skyline.

The day was grand. Hawks wheeled high overhead. Waterfalls thundered into dramatic gorges; canoes, toy-like from the heights, rode the foam. And as I drove through the afternoon proud castles high on rocks seemed to glitter in the sun as though their ramparts were lined with armoured men.

Villages of weathered mellow stone cottages greeted me with brilliant displays of summer blues.

Whenever I stopped I could hear cow bells tinkling over lush meadows. Sun dappled the vineyards, trout fishermen waved from beside clear waters and sails blossomed among the swans on peaceful lakes.

I was seeing the French Jura at its best. And that is saying a great deal. For, to my mind, France has nothing more beautiful and romantic to offer than this natural holiday region 120 miles wide by 180 miles long bounded in the east by Switzerland, in the north by the Vosges, in the south by Savoie and in the west by Burgundy.

Whether you choose it in the spring when the slopes gleam with wild flowers, in the summer when the thermometer climbs so often into the eighties or the autumn when the colours of the landscape are at their loveliest, the area is a delight. By Alpine standards its heights are modest enough – there is little over 5,000 feet. But the plateau I explored on top of Mont d'Or is typical of many quiet reaches high above the valleys.

There is not a vast amount of nightlife in the region – apart from casinos in one or two main centres such as Besançon and some small dance clubs – sophistication is as far away as the world of organized package tours.

But if you yearn for the simple holiday in superb surroundings then the Jura is for you. Bringing your own car from the Channel ports or choosing a fly-drive deal you can have a perfect holiday swimming, windsurfing, sailing, canoeing, playing golf, riding, fishing for trout, pike and carp, climbing and walking, exploring majestic castles and grottoes of bizarre beauty.

And you can stay in a simple country pension charging £10 a day half board, camp on sites where two adults and two children with a car and tent pay £2 a day in fees, or rent a farm cottage for around £70 a week buying your chickens, fruit and vegetables, milk, cream and eggs from the farmer for less than you would pay in the local shops.

There's also a motoring package deal available: a family of four pay £540 for two weeks in a furnished apartment.

Add to reasonable prices and natural beauty a first-rate *cuisine* and the Jura's recipe for holiday bliss is perfect. You will find fondues as good as any you will enjoy in the Alps; some of France's finest charcuterie and cheeses as well as top-class mushroom and trout dishes. And the fruit pastries are a delight.

The most expensive meal of my trip cost me £8 and if there is better value for money anywhere in Europe I will be very surprised. On the night I returned from the heights of Mont d'Or I dined by candlelight in what was once a part of the twelfth-century Abbey of Montbenoit close to the Swiss border and is now a fine restaurant.

First came the delicious full-flavoured smoked ham of the region served with piquant cherries and pickles and hot, crusty bread. Then they brought me mountain mushrooms in cream and wine with croutons, a local speciality.

For my main course there was duckling in a rich sauce of onions and green peppers with savoury meat stuffing and served with peas, beans, tomatoes, lettuce and chicory. There was an impressive selection of regional cheeses; the bilberry tart topped with whipped cream was beautifully light. And the price included coffee and a half-bottle of wine.

It was, as I said, my most expensive meal. More typical of the prices I paid in the region's country restaurants was the ludicrous £3.50 including coffee and a quarter-litre of wine I was charged in a flag-tiled, low-beamed inn at Chissey in the Val d'Amour for charcuterie, veal in cream and wine with feathery dauphine potatoes and peas, carrots and beans, a good cheeseboard and for dessert vacherin – a delicious concoction of home-made cassis and raspberry sorbet with meringue and whipped cream.

There are so many splendid little places to stay, I particularly liked the villages along the Loue Valley, south-east of Besançon – Ornans, for instance, below soaring cliffs where oleander dazzles you in the main square. And idyllic old Vuillafans, perfect for fishing.

There is Lods, where a series of pretty waterfalls lull you to sleep with their soft splashing and Mouthier, where martins circle around the church steeple and wooded mountains seem to rise sheer from the edge of the village.

South-west of Besançon is old-world Arbois nestling among vineyards where you are invited to sample the Jura's fine wines – whites, rosés and rich reds – and walk through a fascinating grotto to see underground falls surging into a quiet river.

If you fancy a water-sports holiday you can stay on the shores of the lovely lake of Saint Point. The local legend says the waters took their colour from the tears of the sad blue-eyed lady of the Castle of Joux.

And there is Besançon itself, the chief town of the region, with its great citadel and ramparts where peacocks and flamingos preen themselves. It is as handsome an old place as you will find anywhere in France.

But of all the castles you can explore in the Jura there are none more majestic than lofty Joux, where sunlight gleams on the swords, breastplates and plumed helmets of the French warriors of old and the view from the battlements is breathtaking.

They take you to the dark little dungeon where the weeping lady with the blue eyes was confined by her jealous husband who decided she had enjoyed his absence at the Crusades in a way not in keeping with the proprieties. Each morning her jailers tantalized her by showing her briefly the beauty of the world outside.

It seemed to me as I stood looking out over those battlements that there must have been many summer mornings when she saw the Jura mist coating the valley and knew that soon the sun would break through. No wonder she shed enough tears to turn a lake blue . . .

Dinner at Montbenoit – Auberge de l'Abbaye.
Dinner at Chissey – Chaumière du Val d'Amour.

5 ROUSSILLON –
THE DEEPEST SOUTH

The peak of mighty Canigou, sacred mountain of the Catalans, was wreathed in cloud and my hotel radio that morning had told of snowfalls in the high Pyrenees.

But the sun had been with me all the way from the Mediterranean shore and I had seen the herald of the Roussillon spring – the first almond blossoms bright against the dark green of the cypress and olive groves.

The steep winding roads from the sea had taken me over wide moorland, between hills terraced with vines. I had bumped over the rough streets of hilltop villages, past sturdy houses with dazzlingly painted shutters and terracotta roofs, their balconies filled with flowers.

The only living creature I had seen for mile after peaceful mile when I left the last village behind was a solitary hawk. Now, high above me, it wheeled at the top of the Galamus Gorge – one of the most spectacular beauty spots in this fascinating holiday region tucked among the mountains of the Corbiere and the Pyrenees and the furthest south you can travel in mainland France.

Overhanging rocks on the narrow road which took me deep inside the gorge formed a huge natural canopy.

But still the sun was warm on my face, gleaming on the tumbling river far below. Halfway through, there was space to turn off the road and I left the car to scramble down a rough path to the river's edge with the simplest of Roussillon country picnics – creamy mountain cheese, olives, bread, and a couple of juicy local oranges.

And sitting there, lulled by the sounds of the little river, I could not help wondering whether so many summer tourists pressing on overcrowded main roads to the nearby Spanish border in search of sun, realized just what they were missing.

Roussillon must be irresistible in summer, with cicadas clicking away in the undergrowth to give notice of yet another warm day, the air sweet with thyme and lavender. France's finest peaches, nectarines and apricots being sold by the roadside at bargain prices – and a warm sea lapping miles of sandy beaches and rocky coves with the thermometer bounding through the eighties and over twelve hours a day sunshine.

But then it wasn't proving too bad in February either . . . I drove out of the gorge with a farewell wave to my friend the hawk and left him to find the crumbs of my lunch. And there was Canigou again, now in full snow-capped glory against a blue sky, the clouds whipped away to reveal the Pyrenees sweeping to the horizon and on to the Costa Brava.

I dined that night beside the Mediterranean in what for me is the most attractive spot on the Roussillon coast – Collioure.

In recent years tourism has come to the region, but nothing can diminish the traditional fishing-village atmosphere of this little place with its impressive mountain background, its pretty harbour, narrow streets and its fine castle.

The red and orange striped flag of the Catalans flies over the castle – you'll see that flag sharing honours with the French tricolor in Roussillon. Centuries ago the region was ruled by Spain and many local people till speak Catalan.

But my dinner in Collioure that moonlit night on my return from the mountains was as French as any Francophile could desire. First, thick creamy fish soup with piquant *rouille* and croutons and grated cheese. Then guinea-fowl cooked slowly to a delicious tenderness in a rich sauce of olives, pimentoes, herbs, onions and mushrooms and served on a bed of rice.

For dessert, I had the house speciality – apple gateau. With coffee and a half-bottle of Roussillon wine I paid £6.50.

Most visitors stay on the coast – there's a sixty-mile shoreline running from the southern tip of Languedoc to the Spanish border and if sandy beaches rather than headlands and rocky coves are essential for your full holiday enjoyment there are twenty-five miles of sands to bask on. The best beaches and the more sophisticated and modern resorts are well to the north of

Collioure – Port Barcares, Canet, St Cyprien, and Argeles.

You can find casinos and a lively nightlife, fine seafood restaurants and handsome palm-fringed waterfronts.

You can sail, water-ski, play tennis and golf, hire horses to ride, fish for bass, bream, and mackerel, join organized tours through the Pyrenees to Andorra or to French beauty spots like Carcassone.

But if old-world charm appeals more than modern sophistication then Collioure is unbeatable. Nearer the Spanish border, Port Vendres and Banyuls – famous for its port-like wine – have a special atmosphere too.

Reckon to pay around £10.50 a day for a small coast hotel with half board and from £4.50 a day in camping fees for a family of four with car and tent. Inland you can hire a family-sized farm cottage from £80 a week and the comparatively few country hotels offer half board from roughly £8 a day.

There are package deals from Britain – a seventeen-day holiday by rail with hotel and breakfast costs £300; a motoring deal for four people sharing a flat for two weeks, works out at £112 per head. A hotel bed and breakfast arrangement for two weeks, travelling by air, comes to about £363. There are also special packages for campers.

To my mind, the freedom a car gives you is the freedom to enjoy Roussillon to the full. The countryside, with its lakes and waterfalls, its views of the Pyrenees and the mountains of the Corbiere sweeping to face each other across the vineyards, is fabulous.

And the entrance to Roussillon's second world is its handsome old capital, Perpignan, just eight miles from the sea.

Try one of the city's many restaurants. I fell for a little place in the heart of town which for £5 served me smooth paté with tiny pickles, olives, and salad; then *moules marinières* followed by a main course of hare cooked in red wine with carrots, bacon, mushrooms, and onions; and for dessert a fine fruit tart. And the price included coffee and a quarter-litre of wine.

President Mitterrand, as all Heads of State before him, has a yearly sweet reminder of Roussillon's loyalty to France – the first of the season's cherries from the countryside around Ceret, a romantic old place in the far south of the region. Ceret is filled with memories of Picasso, who admired the town so much, and with the streets lined with the most magnificent plane trees I have ever seen.

I ate in a delightful inn with stunning views from its terrace, at the idyllic hilltop village of Castelnou. The host is renowned as a hunter and though it meant paying slightly more than for other main dishes on his menu I could not resist the wild boar in red wine which he served after fine charcuterie and an omelette filled with big juicy mountain mushrooms.

With a dessert of his wife's meltingly light patisserie, with coffee and a half-bottle of house wine, I paid £8.50.

In the north of the region, close to what was once the Spanish–French frontier, stands the great castle of Salses. And nearby is a monument marking the scene of the last attempt by Spain to regain Roussillon.

Spanish troops were pushed back to the south with heavy losses. And the region, for all its Catalan flags and traditions, has been firmly French ever since.

But stand there on those castle ramparts with the quiet beauty of the place around you and you'll feel you couldn't blame the Spaniards for wanting Roussillon back.

It is a treasure for any nation to possess.

Dinner at Collioure – La Bodega, 6 Rue de la Republique.
Dinner at Perpignan – La Casserole, 1 Place des Varietes.
Meal at Castelnou – L'Hostal restaurant.

6 LITTLE MAYENNE

It was the best of all ways to prove how easy it is to find the real, timeless France. A turn off the noisy highway south and there it was . . .

Suddenly I had the road to myself – a narrow winding road running past cherry and peach orchards, through sleepy villages of sturdy granite cottages, past rambling farmhouses backed by a sweep of wooded hills, a glimpse of a pinnacled château snug in sun-dappled oak and chestnut groves.

Even the weather seemed to have cheered up. The drizzle which had followed me from Cherbourg was gone.

I wound down the car window to breathe air free of petrol fumes, waved to a rosy-cheeked girl leading cows from a field and to a group of anglers at a lakeside and felt I had found summer all over again.

Until that turn-off the highway, Mayenne had been a mere name to me, a *département* you pass through at speed bound for more glamorous destinations. Now I was finding its charm for the first time.

It is only a little piece of France beyond the Normandy border and marking the edge of the western Loire, just sixty miles from north to south and forty east to west. But small as it is, Mayenne has everything that makes a French country holiday perfection.

And even if the sea is within reach if you take your own car and stay in Mayenne, Mont St Michel is a mere thirty miles from its north-western boundary, the beaches of La Baule are an easy drive away, while the glories of the Loire châteaux are just sixty miles from the region's centre.

There are lakes and rivers ideal for swimming, canoeing, windsurfing, sailing, water-skiing and trout and carp fishing. There are lovely old castles to explore and miles of forests. You can play golf and tennis and hire a horse.

As for the food . . . the closeness of Normandy and Brittany combined with the finesse of local chefs ensures marvellously prepared seafood and fish dishes in scores of little restaurants often for a fraction of what you would pay in a coastal resort.

With one cow per head of population, the cream is thick and lavish. And the most modest character in Mayenne insists that the region's calvados, cider, camembert and Breton-style pancakes are easily as good as the originals.

Mayenne *cuisine* is simply glorious. That was plain to me at my very first lunch. I stopped in a peaceful little spot called St Pierre des Nids and chose a small hotel.

My lunch cost me £7. With my aperitif of white wine and cassis I was served appetizers of quiche lorraine and plums wrapped in bacon. There was creamy home-made pork and veal terrine, a superb main course of guinea-fowl cooked in cider with mushrooms and ham and served with mixed vegetables, and for dessert I had the house speciality – an apple soaked in calvados and topped by a sorbet that would not have disgraced a first-class chef in Paris. And the price included coffee and a half-litre of wine.

There are so many little hotels like the place I chose. Reckon on an average half-board price of £10.

For instance, stay in Saulges – a perch and trout fisherman's dream where waterfalls sparkle below Dordogne-like cliffs.

There is peaceful little Neau where I dined one night on five courses with wine and coffee for just £7 and the unforgettable main dish was quail cooked with butter and mushrooms.

There is St Ceneri deep in a wooded valley with the river Sarthe running through its heart. And Ambrieres, near the largest lake of the region and where you can eat delicious seafood for £6 including wine and coffee.

My dinner began with a dish of six oysters with herb filling, followed by a skate with black butter, capers, salad and a fresh lemon garnish. There was the usual fine cheeseboard and for dessert, profiteroles – rich with hot chocolate, ice cream and almonds.

If you prefer to stay in a town with some nightlife – although even in main centres don't reckon on anything more than a few little dance clubs – you can make your choice of three spots on the Mayenne river; Mayenne itself, Château Gontier and the region's capital, Laval.

And Laval, where the river is spanned by graceful bridges, has more than a touch of Paris in miniature with its sweeping tree-lined river front bordered by stately houses. Mayenne also stages colourful spectacles for its visitors.

One night under the moon I took my seat on the shore of a lake where swans glided. Suddenly, brilliantly coloured fountains spurted high, the majestic castle of Lassay on the far shore glowed with light and armoured knights, plumes waving, thundered at each other in a tournament.

Musketeers fought a mock battle, swords clashed, beautiful women with sweeping pre-Revolution gowns alighted from a coach complete with bewigged attendants.

And the whole history of Lassay was enacted in a unique mixture of *son et lumière* and pageant.

Not that Mayenne and its main river needs a staged spectacle to capture you. The Mayenne river meanders gently among watermills, wooded islands and high locks operated by pretty girls. You can take boat trips, hire cabin cruisers and if you come with a caravan, you can even hire a flat-bottomed barge on which you drive your caravan, chug away to a secluded mooring and thus have a house-boat holiday with a difference.

There are also camp sites where a family of four with caravan pay from £4.50 a day in fees and country cottages to be hired for about £120 for two weeks.

I have two outstanding memories of my Mayenne visit. One is of walking under a green canopy of boughs through which sunlight filtered and finding in a clearing a young couple kneeling hand in hand to drink from a spring of crystal water. For centuries the people of Mayenne have come to that spring to make a wish for future happiness.

And the second memory? Although Mayenne is not a place for sadness the experience was poignant.

From the hamlet of Champs Fremont to a spot on the edge of the forest a road winds through the meadows for just over a mile. I made that walk on a lovely summer day with the hedgerows bright with foxgloves, the air filled with birdsong and the sound of my footsteps echoing through the silence.

On such a perfect day in 1944 the Germans rounded up a group of Maquis fighters and marched them along that road to a spot chosen for execution. At the last moment a few managed to break free and escape into the forest, but others were not fast enough. And at the end of the road a simple memorial records their martyrdom.

Walking that road so many years later I could not help wondering whether those young men looked around at the peaceful charm of their Mayenne and realized just how much they had to live for. And whether to the survivors, Mayenne seemed even more beautiful when they finally emerged from the forest to the sunlight of freedom.

Lunch at Saint Pierre des Nids – Hotel du Dauphin.
Meal at Ambrieres – Le Gue-de-Genes.
Meal at Neau – Hotel-Restaurant de la Croix Verte.

7 THE PARIS WINTER WEEKEND

My coach from the Gare du Nord drove through the thronged Pigalle and along the great boulevard at the foot of the most famous of all Paris hills.

Then we began the steep climb on Montmartre cobble stones with Sacré Coeur etched against the late afternoon sky in ornate splendour over the house tops ahead.

Minutes later I was following the proprietor of my winter weekend hotel up a winding staircase to a cosy little room high in the eaves. The view from my window was magnificent.

All Paris lay at my feet and I was seeing it at a magic time of the day when the first lights were springing up and at a very special time of the week in the world's most romantic city – Friday afternoon.

The Eiffel Tower soared on the horizon with the modernistic Montparnasse tower sharing the skyline. The Grand Palais, the Opera, the Pantheon and Les Invalides domes – I could see them all from my little room.

Montmartre itself captured me on that first night. First a stroll to the Place Tertre for a drink and to see the artists at work among the trees, to hear the first strumming of guitars as the strolling musicians tuned up for the evening.

Then a visit to Sacré Coeur, dominating the hilltop and now enhanced by floodlights and looking more like a wedding cake than ever.

And dinner at the Rue Caulaincourt by candlelight with the pictures painted by those Montmartre artists on the walls in a fine little bistro and with food and setting so Parisian as to remove any doubts I may still have felt that a journey of seven and a half hours by rail and hovercraft from London in winter was eminently worthwhile.

They brought me smooth turkey paté followed by *moules marinière*, a main dish of tender chunks of beef in a rich red wine sauce with tomatoes, onions and peppers and a light pasta and for dessert profiteroles as only the French know how to prepare. With coffee and a half-litre of wine I paid £8.

Feeling marvellous, I walked back up the hill to gaze out over the terrace to see Paris – now a blaze of light – looking even more beautiful. The square throbbed with music and echoed with laughter and the cheerful chink of glasses from restaurants and cafes.

I squeezed into a bar, ordered a beer, listened to a girl singing with all the gusto of Piaf herself, beat time to Country and Western numbers, banged the table like everyone else for a husky repeat of an Aznavour favourite and felt so much part of the scene that when I glanced at my watch we were already well into Saturday.

I had begun my Paris weekend by taking the morning boat train from Charing Cross on Friday; the hovercraft had sped me across the Channel in forty minutes to connect with the Paris train. That cosy room in Montmartre complete with breakfast was mine for two nights. And Paris was mine until I left reluctantly on Sunday afternoon to be back in London by 8 p.m.

The basic cost of the package deal I chose was £63. To this you must add your main meals, your entertainment and all other extras in the city which lives up to its reputation for high prices.

But Paris is worth it.

Go in winter and however well you think you know your Paris you will look with new eyes and find yourself envying people there for the first time.

And although some high costs are unavoidable you can still save yourself unnecessary expense by ignoring pricey, organized excursions and sightseeing.

You can arm yourself with a map and buy a £4 ticket entitling you to unlimited Metro and bus travel for two days and enjoy without being jostled so many of the sights you saw when you first went to Paris.

The Metro was fifty yards from my hotel – it could take me to the Opera in ten minutes and to Concorde in fifteen on Saturday

morning. I chose Concorde and thought the great square with fountains and the matchless sweep of the Champs Elysées all aglow with winter sunshine filling the crisp air, was at its very best.

The elegance of the Rue de Rivoli, the loveliness of the Tuileries Gardens, the fascination of the Louvre with the Winged Victory and the Mona Lisa, the lovers' walks by the Seine . . . the charm of Paris was all around me that weekend.

I found a new free attraction – the courtyard of the Pompidou Centre filled with life and colour: clowns with painted faces juggling before a delighted audience, fire-eaters leaving children wide-eyed with wonder, guitarists persuading the onlookers to sing with them, actors rehearsing a play oblivious of the crowds around them . . .

In the Rue Bonaparte opposite the School of Fine Arts I lunched in an old-world bistro complete with mirrored walls, marble-topped tables and red checkered cloths.

There was charcuterie with lots of crusty bread as a starter. My main course was the perfect French dish for an appetite sharpened by a long walk on a nippy day – a warming meat and vegetable concoction *pot au feu*. For dessert a light apple and mirabelle tart. And the price with coffee and a quarter-litre of wine – a mere £3.80.

My boat trip on the Seine from the nearby Pont Neuf was a bargain too – £1.70 for an hour on waters sparkling with sunshine; with the winged horsemen on the Pont Alexandre III gleaming as though Paris had just polished them up in your honour and the lovely buildings you pass drowsing in the glow of the afternoon.

I watched the sunset through the magnificent stained-glass windows of Notre Dame and then left the peace of the Ile de la Cité and walked through the Latin Quarter livening up for Saturday night.

On the edge of the Quarter, I dined beneath the chandeliers of a restaurant in the Rue de L'Ancienne Comédie, which has dispensed marvellous food and hospitality since the days of Louis XIV. I chose a light *vol au vent* filled with Rocquefort cheese and a pair of plump full-flavoured quail cooked with white wine and grapes and served with croutons.

The cheese was splendid and my dessert, *omelet Norwegienne*, filled with ice cream and topped with meringue, was flamed with brandy at the table. With coffee and a half-bottle of wine my bill came to £10 and I did not think I was overcharged.

The Champs Elysées gleaming with light claimed me for the most expensive extra in the entire weekend. But then a Saturday night in Paris without a glittering show would be a sin.

I chose the Lido and for two hours saw a dazzling spectacular of gorgeous girls in plumed sequins, conjurors and acrobats and ballet and folk dancing in fantastic costumes and with so many change of scenery and lighting effects you wonder how it is done.

I drank the only stuff you should drink in a top-rate Paris nightclub – champagne. The half-bottle they brought me came as part of the entrance fee I paid – £21.25. And that is the minimum you will pay in any top Paris show.

Extravagant? Of course, but the show combined with the champagne made me feel so delighted with my Paris weekend and convinced me that nightclubs virtually everywhere else are pale imitations.

Paris on Sunday morning out of season has a quiet charm of its own. I paid my respects to Napoleon lying in Les Invalides.

I took the lift high up the Eiffel Tower for the most famous of all Paris views. Below me the green velvet lawns of the Champs de Mars were speckled with the last fallen leaves of the year and I could not resist a last wistful look at the distant Sacré Coeur brooding on the Montmartre hill.

Then there was just time for a last stroll along the Seine and lunch in a pleasant little restaurant in the Place Charles Michels.

It was a delicious meal: a starter of nuts, smoked bacon, coleslaw and onions with a subtle dressing; a main dish of a huge steak in a pepper and cream sauce with mixed vegetables followed by a generous slice of blueberry tart with lashings of cream. And the cost with coffee and a quarter-litre of wine? Just over £5.

As I said, you will find yourself envying people who are seeing Paris for the first time. But by spending a weekend there out of the main holiday season a lover of Paris is doing the next best thing.

Hotel – Bouquet de Montmartre.
Friday dinner – Au Tournant de la Butte, Rue Caulaincourt.
Saturday lunch – Restaurant des Beaux-Arts, Rue Bonaparte.
Saturday dinner – Café Procope, Rue de l'Ancienne-Comédie.
Sunday lunch – Le Patio, Place Charles Michels.

8   THE LOIRE VALLEY

It was the perfect spot to pick for my evening in Orleans at the start of three off-season days of French enchantment.

The waiter led me to a table by a window overlooking the square in the heart of the city where old-fashioned street lamps cast a soft glow on the facades of handsome buildings and seemed to mellow even the fierceness of an armoured Joan of Arc astride her horse.

Perfect. An evening for romance when even the deadliest enemies could be reconciled. I wished I could have invited the Maid of Orleans to dinner . . .

As it was I could only raise my glass of Touraine wine to her in silent tribute. I was sitting among the decorative palms under the gleaming white canopy of one of the parasols stretching over the tables in a fashionable Belle Epoque-style restaurant.

My wine came straight from the keg and I could help myself to as much as I liked, at no extra cost. The hors d'oeuvre were unlimited too – a great buffet of smoked eels and mackerel, quiches, mushrooms from the Loire Valley woods and meadows, superb ham, patés, and sausages, artichokes, aubergines and salads with subtle garnishes.

My main course, local lamb, came spitted with onions and peppers and was served with delicately flavoured rice. And for dessert I chose with difficulty, from a table laden with good things, a meltingly light chocolate charlotte. And complete with coffee and tip my feast – for feast it was – cost me £7.

It felt so good to be there to relax at the end of my drive from the ferry terminal at Le Havre, to sip my wine and look forward to the next few days in the Loire Valley, to the winding roads through vineyards and orchards so quiet when the main tourist season is over, to see the loveliest châteaux in all France soaring above the forests where kings and cavaliers once hunted.

And to gaze down from graceful bridges over the river at the heart of it all.

I had chosen a £68 package deal offered by a cross-Channel ferry company which gave me freedom to enjoy the Loire Valley at my own pace.

The basic cost for each of two people gives the choice of bringing your car on any day of the week on the short crossing from Dover to Bolougne with a longer drive to the Loire region or the lengthier journey from Southampton to Le Havre which cuts down the amount of mileage facing you on the Continent. You also have three nights' bed and breakfast in modern comfortable hotels with private bath at Orleans, Blois and Tours.

You can spend all three nights in one town or you can do as I did and book yourself for a night in each. I also found it worth paying a small supplement to take the night crossing from Southampton so that after an easy morning's drive you can arrive in Orleans in early afternoon and enjoy the maximum time in the region.

Choose a weekend, for example, and you can end your journey from the ferry on Friday afternoon and not have to begin driving back to the coast to pick up the night boat home until after lunch on Monday. If you want to pay for extra luxury, there's a special offer of a grand four-star hotel at Tours.

Even when frost glitters on the pinnacled towers of the châteaux and the carpet of leaves on the great lawns is crisp underfoot there's a magic in the air. Each of the cities where you stay also has a special charm. There's Orleans with its stateliness, the cathedral where Joan of Arc came in triumph after saving the city from the English and, nearby, her lovingly restored timber-framed house.

At Blois the streets rise steeply between rows of ancient houses and the great château broods above. And there's Tours, where away from the bustle of the main avenue you can find a timeless world of cobbled squares and old houses which seem to lean towards each other.

You don't go looking for nightlife although there are a few dance clubs in the main centres and Tours has a famous and

elegant theatre offering ballet, opera and concerts. You can also
fish for carp and pike, play a round of golf or go riding.

But you are more likely just to let the spell of the place take
you over in its own effortless way. And the beauty of a deal like
this is that it allows you to spend each day without a rigid plan.

I remember the night I was booked in at Tours. I had planned
to dine out there in an old quarter famous for its gourmet
restaurants. I had picnicked in my car on the banks of the Loire
and then driven to perhaps the most beautiful old town in the
region – Chinon, dominated by a castle from which knights
once rode to the Crusades.

I lingered there watching the sun go down and the moon rise
over the castle and nothing seemed more appealing than dining
there before I moved into the big city.

And what a joy that dinner was. First they brought me *rillette*,
the full-flavoured terrine-like pork speciality of the region
served in a tiny earthenware bowl and accompanied by little
pickles. Then a masterpiece to my mind – *quenelles* of Loire pike
topped with cheese served with mushrooms and a rich delicious
crayfish cream and pepper sauce.

There was a fine cheese selection to follow and, for dessert, an
apple and caramel flan. With coffee and a half-bottle of house
wine I was charged just £8.

You don't have to be a history buff to steep yourself in the
atmosphere of the tapestried Loire châteaux when you visit them
out of season.

The glory of Usse, everyone's idea of a fairyland castle, is that
it was the setting of the legend of the Sleeping Beauty. Go there
in winter and it is so wrapped in peace that you feel the lady
should sleep on, undisturbed even by the gentle kiss of the
prince who awakens her from enchantment.

I loved the simplicity mingled with the grandeur – the
morning mist rising as I drove through the great hunting forest,
the Chambord; the sleepy flutter of doves' wings; the swans
ruffling their plumage on the lake and the deer watching me
bright-eyed from among the trees.

I remember the fountains which tinkled away in the
Versailles-like terraced gardens of Villandry; and the splash of

the waterfalls almost under the windows of Azay lying in majesty on its island in the Indre river.

I remember too the great banners of chivalry bright with fleur-de-lys flying from the battlements of Amboise. Far below you, the Loire creams beneath the town bridge, on the horizon the wooded hills sweep into the distance.

But most vividly of all I shall remember Chenonceaux, to my mind the loveliest building in France with its poignant memories of the ill-fated Mary Stuart when she was the French Queen and its gallery resting on slender arches spanning the river Cher and filled with the soft strains of period background music.

I could not have chosen a better moment. On an afternoon so quiet that I could hear my own footsteps on the tiled floor of that gallery lined with orange trees, I felt that if I closed my eyes I could see the kings and queens and nobles of old gazing through the windows at the forest, green river banks and the flowers still blooming in the château gardens.

The only other visitor there, an American, was as much under the spell of the place as I was. He shook his head in wonderment. 'How for Pete's sake do I tell them at home about all this?' he asked me.

'They'll never believe you,' I told him.

Dinner in Orleans – L'Assiette.
Meal at Chinon – Le Sainte Maxime restaurant.
Dinner at Blois – Hotel Le Monarque.

9 ICI COMMENCE LA NORMANDIE – *DIEPPE*

The joy of a winter weekend in France . . . for me it began past the anglers on the Dieppe jetty, past the sign adorned with golden lions over the ferry terminal: '*Ici commence la Normandie.*'

I found it behind the arcaded waterfront in the shadow of the magnificent cliff-top château.

It was three minutes from the harbour. And I relished it without a backward glance at the sleek Paris boat train which claimed most of my fellow travellers crossing from Newhaven that Friday afternoon. The shop windows in the Grande Rue were so tempting – filled with marvellous cheeses, patés, cakes, and long fragrant loaves.

The joy of France – and the sweetness of it there for the tasting. Those patisseries proved irresistible. Such delights – éclairs topped with coffee cream, chocolate gateaux coated with bilberries, apple cake as only the Normans can make it, rich with calvados.

I settled for a superb creation of almonds, fruit, cream and the lightest sponge flavoured with Grand Marnier, sipped first-rate coffee and envied no one on that train to Paris. And I was just sixty miles from England.

I wandered happily through the town past the fishing harbour and the nets and baskets and the burly, sweatered types handling them.

I climbed the battlements of that graceful château for a view over the rooftops to the green Norman hills beyond and explored the lofty rooms inside filled with all the salty treasures you'd expect to find in a French stronghold guarding the Channel shore.

There were ships in bottles, magnificent models of men-of-war, relics of seamen who fought us in battles of long ago and,

more surprisingly, the delicate ivory works of Dieppe's old craftsmen and the paintings, many by British artists, of the long-vanished bathing-machine world of Dieppe at the turn of the century.

They had switched on the floodlights at the cathedral by the time I emerged and lights were twinkling by the shore. Time to check in at my hotel where I was to stay for two nights – it was just minutes from the sea and the shopping streets.

And the room they gave me, complete with private bath, was both spacious and cosy – the sort of French hotel room that I found next morning was at its best filled with sunshine, the cry of gulls from the town roofs calling laggards out of bed and the aroma of breakfast coffee and newly-baked croissants.

I had chosen Dieppe for a package deal weekend. The £47 you pay – what tremendous value this is – gives you two nights at the hotel with breakfast, the round trip from Newhaven, the return rail fare from any station in Kent or Sussex and reduced fares from many other British stations.

If you can't spare more than one night, you pay just £34.50, but Dieppe, with its old-fashioned charm, its superb low-priced hypermarket shopping, its setting and its magnificent seafood, is so attractive, so much more than just a ferry transit port that it deserves two nights at the very least.

Another attraction of the deal is that you can go on any day of the week and on any Sealink ferry crossing. But to make a weekend of it starting for home on Sunday afternoon is to my mind the best choice of all.

I could have eaten more cheaply elsewhere but I was determined to start my Dieppe weekend in style and the elegance of the restaurant on the Quai Henry IV yards from the ferry terminal proved a perfect choice. Dinner cost me £9 including service, coffee and a half-bottle of Muscadet.

And how fine it was. I had fish soup served with grated cheese, croutons and piquant rouille sauce; skate in mustard and cream; a big selection of Normandy cheeses and for dessert a delicious almond charlotte.

Later I joined fellow visitors in Dieppe's best-known meeting spot, a softly-lit bar in the heart of town where the background music was soft enough not to irritate. We relaxed on comfortable leather benches and the atmosphere was so pleasant that somehow we did not mind paying slightly more for our drinks than in an ordinary cafe – a glass of wine or a beer for about 60p.

On Saturday morning Dieppe transforms itself from a port to a country market town with all the produce of the Norman countryside set out by farmers and growers who virtually take the place over. They bring rural Normandy to you but there's no substitute for exploring it yourself and after a look round at the market square that is just what I did.

You can have a pleasant weekend in Dieppe without a car. You can play golf, go fishing or hire a horse. If you want a change of scene for a few hours, you can take the train to beautiful old Rouen where the heart of our Crusader king, Richard I, is buried in the cathedral. And you can walk in winter sunshine across the great square where we martyred Joan of Arc.

But at a time of the year when the quiet Norman roads are a motorist's delight and buses are infrequent, there's nothing to beat taking your own car – well worth the extra £15 you are charged on the round ferry trip.

So on Saturday afternoon and Sunday morning I drove through some of the most attractive regions of Normandy along the coast to peaceful little Veules les Roses, left my car for a bracing walk along the beach under towering cliffs and then headed through the pinewoods to St Marguerite, where the view from the lighthouse is breathtaking.

I climbed the steep hill to the great royal castle of Arques la Bataille with Normandy stretching at my feet, and in the winter stillness I could almost hear the hoofbeats of armoured knights riding out to combat. I fell for little Cleres where a river runs through the heart of town, and Luneray, one of the prettiest villages in Normandy and famous for its colourful Sunday-morning market. I explored the valley of the Saane – a valley filled with rustling beech forests, stately châteaux and rambling old timber-framed farmhouses.

And at the sleepy village of Auzouville sur Saane I lunched on Saturday beneath the venerable seventeenth-century beams of what was once the local school, now transformed into a cosy auberge. I chose Norman country fare at its best: a starter of smooth duck terrine; quenelles of pike with salad and a fine sauce; hare in red wine, tender and delicious; cheese and for dessert a light apricot pudding.

With coffee, service and a quarter-litre of wine, it all cost me £7.90.

But the gastronomic high spot of my weekend was served that night by candlelight in Dieppe itself. With the town's classic dish, Marmite Dieppoise, you don't need a starter and a refreshing lemon sorbet served in a hollowed-out lemon to add taste proved just right as a dessert.

Marmite Dieppoise is a meal in itself – mixed scallops, langoustines, mussels, skate, turbot and angler fish sizzling before you on a little burner and all in a cream and wine sauce ideal for mopping up with that inimitable French bread. I paid just less than £9 for that a la carte meal in a leading restaurant, the price including service, coffee and a half-bottle of wine.

Later I had the choice of ending my evening in a friendly little bar, visiting the plush casino or meeting fellow Britons in the casino's elegant dance club with British disc jockeys who are happy to oblige with any number from tangos and Beatles and rock 'n' roll to the latest hits.

I chose the disco, paid just over £5 for admission and one drink and £2.50 for further drinks and, like everyone else, barely noticed the early hours of Sunday slipping away.

After my Sunday-morning country drive I was back in Dieppe for the last meal of my weekend, another fine fish and seafood lunch almost within sight of the ferry terminal.

Later, sailing home past the sign which tells you that Normandy begins with Dieppe, I reflected wistfully that it ends there too. But there was one consoling thought – it is so delightfully easy to go back and fall in love with Dieppe and Normandy all over again.

Hotel – Select.
Coffee and cakes on arrival – Divernet Salon.
Friday dinner – La Musardière.
Saturday lunch – At Auzouville sur Saane – Auberge au Bord de la Saane.
Saturday dinner – La Marmite Dieppoise.
Sunday lunch – Les Tourelles.

10 CASSIS – PROVENCE UNDER WINTER SKIES

Nothing stirred on the heights of Cap Canaille that glorious autumn day except the slightest breeze from the Mediterranean shimmering 1,300 feet below, rustling the heather. The only sound was the chirp of crickets in the umbrella pines.

For me Saturday afternoon under cloudless Provençale skies on top of Europe's highest cliff was the perfect start to a weekend of southern French magic.

Inland the mountains rolled away to the horizon. Ahead of me the Mediterranean had never seemed so blue. And in its little bay to my right and surrounded by banks of oleander and pine groves, Cassis drowsed in the sun.

It still had its late-season tourists swimming, skin-diving and relaxing in waterfront cafes. But at the end of the winding road from the town to the heights I had the mighty cape to myself.

Marseilles Airport, a mere thirty miles distant, could have been on the other side of the world. And London, where I had taken off that morning for a flight of eighty minutes, seemed a lifetime away.

I watched the headland across the bay grow pink in about the most spectacular sunset you can see anywhere in Europe, the boats were heading back to Cassis for the night, the first lights began to twinkle in the town. And I knew it was time to go down for an aperitif and dinner.

The Renault 5 with which I took that steep road back to Cassis was mine with unlimited mileage until I drove back to Marseilles Airport to catch the Tuesday-afternoon plane home. Like my comfortable hotel room with private shower and a view of one of the most attractive little harbours anywhere on the French Mediterranean shore, that car was part of an off-season bed and breakfast deal including the round flight from Heathrow.

It is not the cheapest deal you can find if you yearn for a brief escape from a British autumn and winter – it operates until the end of March and costs from £168.

To the basic price you must add your main meals, your entertainment and the bill for petrol in a region which lives up to its reputation for being one of the most expensive in France.

But the special charms of the place in the off-season months are a climate which even in mid-winter is so often like a good British spring, the beauty of the surroundings and that inimitable French food.

I dined on full-flavoured fish soup with croutons, grated cheese and a creamy piquant sauce to add. Then came bream cooked to perfection with fennel and a mustard and egg sauce. My dessert was a feathery light lemon tart. With coffee and a half-bottle of Cassis wine that meal cost me over £8 – I could have eaten more cheaply elsewhere but deliberately chose a first-class restaurant to start my weekend in style.

A nightcap in the little bar on the quay, a stroll past brightly painted houses with flower-filled balconies and listening to the languid notes of a guitar serenade from one of the little bars by the waterside, was for me far more satisfying than a visit to a casino or dance club and little Cassis can provide these too if you want them.

Your Cassis-based weekend can be as full and active as you care to make it – you can fish, sail, water-ski, windsurf, skin-dive. And even in mid-winter when only the hardiest types swim you can sun yourself on the rocks and the tiny beaches nearby for long enough to get a tan.

And with the freedom a car gives you, the lovely old cities of Arles and Avignon, the glamour of St Tropez, the charm of the Camargue and the famous gorges of the south are all within easy reach.

My Sunday started with a forty-five-minute motor-launch trip for £1.50 through the Calanques, the fiord-like inlets where limestone cliffs soar hundreds of feet above you and the waters are so clear that you can see every movement of the skin-divers below. Then I drove across the Massif Saint-Baume to the north-east, past huge forests and sleepy hilltop villages and down again to the soft green of vineyards.

In the main square of Saint Maximum I stopped for lunch, my appetite sharpened by a combination of mountain and sea air. The little inn I chose proudly proclaimed itself to be the scene of the wedding in 1794 of Napoleon's brother Lucien to the innkeeper's sister.

All I can tell you is that the lunch they served me would have satisfied even that lady's famous brother-in-law. None of your paper-thin slivers of country ham as a starter – but thick juicy slices served with olives. Then came trout with a champagne sauce on a bed of rice.

My main course – chosen with difficulty from a yard-long menu that offered every type of game including pheasant, guinea-fowl and hare – was tender wild boar. There was a fine cheese selection and for dessert an ice cream meringue gateau topped with whipped cream.

With coffee and a half-bottle of wine my lunch cost me £7 and sent me on my way feeling like an emperor.

I drove an easy few miles to Aix, handsome old capital of Provence, strolled among the students sunning themselves in the open-air cafes on the tree-lined Cours Mirabeau, sampled the local sweet speciality – cakes of almond and crystallized melon called calissons with coffee in a cafe near the lovely old clock tower in the heart of town.

When I saw the Mediterranean again it was from the mellow stone walls of Le Castellet, a hilltop village where the houses are hung with clematis, honeysuckle, bougainvillaea and oleander. And I drove back to Cassis happy at the prospect of another seafront meal.

The neighbouring resorts of Bandol and Sanary were bright with early-morning sunshine gilding their seafront palms when I drove the coast road on Monday heading for Toulon.

For one of the most magnificent harbour views in all France I took the cable car up Mont Faron. From the battlements of the beflagged castle, now an impressive monument to the men who fought in the 'forgotten D-Day' – the Allied landings in southern France in the summer of 1944 – I looked out over the vine terraces and valleys of the wild country just inland from the city.

Toulon has a fascinating old quarter with leafy squares where fountains play and a naval museum with fine models of the men-of-war which once fought us for mastery of the Channel.

It is also a first-class place for a hungry motorist. I chose a pleasant little restaurant in the Place Puget complete with Belle Epoque lamps, cane furniture and potted palms.

They served me shrimps in a creamy sauce with rice and sultanas, then lamb Provençale style with herbs and ratatouille and, for dessert, a fine pineapple marzipan rum and cream gateau.

The crusty bread was studded with walnuts – an imaginative touch to say the least. And the price with coffee and a quarter-litre of wine? Just £6.

I took a twenty-minute ferry journey to a more peaceful world – to the island of Porquerolles. They won't have cars from the mainland there but you can hire a bicycle and ride off beside a lovely beach fringed by pinewoods or you can do as I did – simply take a walk with the sun on your face and feel glad to be there.

That night I dined in an elegant hotel restaurant just off the harbour at Cassis. And I paid £7, starting with mussels, green peppers and mushrooms cooked and served on a spit – absolutely delicious. A pair of plump red mullet came next served with a crisp salad.

For dessert I chose little Grand Marnier pancakes. And the price included coffee and a half-bottle of Cassis wine.

Lunch next day was merely a picnic of bread, olives, paté, cheese, fruits and a half-bottle of wine. But the setting was magnificent. Once again I had the summit of Cap Canaille to myself. Once again the crickets in the pine trees chirped a welcome. But my suitcase was in the car boot and I thought wistfully that long before another super sunset I would be back in London.

A *long* weekend did I say? I've never known days pass so quickly.

Hotel – Cassitel.
Saturday dinner – La Vieille Auberge Restaurant.
Sunday lunch – Le Relais Bonaparte at St Maximin-la-Ste-Baume.
Sunday dinner – Not stated.
Monday lunch – Le Jardin des Délices, Place Puget, Toulon.
Monday dinner – Le Provençal Hotel Restaurant, Cassis.
Tuesday lunch – Picnic.

11 CANNES WHEN THE TOURISTS HAVE GONE

Time to go back to Entrevaux's tiny station for the return leg of one of the most spectacular, romantic railway trips you can make anywhere in Europe . . .

I took a last look at the old town of fairytale beauty 1,400 feet up among the Alps of Provence – at the medieval streets wrapped in winter stillness but flooded with sunshine, at the great castle brooding high above me, reached by a fantastic steep zig-zag fortified causeway I had climbed for a marvellous view that morning.

I walked past the little restaurant beside the ancient olive mill where I had lunched on four courses with wine and coffee and including splendid mountain trout for just over £6.

And then, rattling and swaying as it burst out of the tunnel penetrating the olive-coated mountain slope, came my train back to the Mediterranean shore – a one-carriage diesel.

Once again I marvelled at the ever-changing scenery. I watched through its windows as Entrevaux vanished: dramatic gorges with the Var flowing through their heart, old villages clinging to the mountainsides. The clouds around the peaks whipped away in a refreshing breeze, the sun broke through again. Orchards and vineyards in softer, greener countryside passed as we descended.

And there before me, with dramatic suddenness, gleaming in the soft dusk, the lights of the Promenade des Anglais springing up beside the sea, was – Nice.

I changed to a bigger train for the last few miles of a 120-mile day excursion which had taken me from Cannes to the Alpes du Sud by normal public service – the tiny mountain railway serves the country villages – and cost me just £8 in fares. The very direction signs I passed now spelt Riviera glamour in them-

A romantic railway trip from Cannes . . . the fairytale village of Entrevaux

selves: Antibes, Juan Les Pins, St Tropez.

I remembered then the soft purr of the black, long sleek saloon car which had collected me from Nice Airport when I flew in from London winter chill to Cote d'Azur sunshine at the start of my off-season week in Cannes – all part of the service you get when you choose a package deal holiday like mine on the Riviera.

I felt almost like purring myself that day for the sheer pleasure of being there under blue skies with the thermometer hovering around sixty and with winter kept safely at bay on the far side of the snow-capped Alpes du Sud.

Now, back from that fantastic railway trip, I felt just as happy to see the coastline again. Soon I was at my simple but comfortable little hotel high in the Old Town of Cannes, with my window overlooking a garden filled with palms, orange and medlar trees.

There are less pricey ways of spending a winter or early-spring week – flying by scheduled service from London on any day you choose and staying in an hotel with breakfast and private bath, costs just over £200. To this you must add your meals, entertainment and local travel; but while it is all too easy to spend a small fortune there are so many ways of passing a splendid week on the Riviera without too much strain on your pocket.

Anyway, money can't buy the charms of a Riviera holiday in the off-season. This is a delightfully different Cannes from the Cannes of the international film festival.

The luxury cabin cruisers and yachts are silent at their moorings, the opulent summer crowds have vanished, the famous palm-fringed Croisette is yours to stroll.

This is the Cannes of the fabulous winter sunsets, when the honey-coloured buildings of the hilly Old Town deepen in rich pink before the onset of dusk and then glow with soft floodlighting under the stars and the rising moon.

You don't have to be a millionaire to dine out well. Minutes from the Croisette I found a pleasant little restaurant which served me rich and creamy fish soup with grated cheese, croutons and piquant rouille, followed by delicious bass garnished with lemon and served with cannelloni – the Italian influence is strong here.

Then came a fine cheese selection and superb profiteroles. The half-litre of wine was just right and so was the coffee. And the price, including service, was no more than I paid for that simple country meal at Entrevaux – just over £6.

On another evening, for about £2 more, I dined on the Croisette itself in a delightful candlelit restaurant built like a summer pavilion.

Beef in wine, cream and shallots was the main dish of my three-course meal with wine and coffee. For dessert there was a masterpiece of a gateau – made with chocolate mousse, vanilla cream, the airiest of sponge cakes topped with mocha and slivers of white chocolate. I ate to a soft serenade by strolling troubadours with guitar and violin.

Nightlife? There are cosy little bars where you can sip a glass of wine for 6op, piano bars where drinks are pricier but sentimental music is a pleasure to hear as you relax after a day in the sun, discos charging £6 for admission and one drink. And much better value for money – a pleasant little cabaret with a Paris-type floorshow in miniature followed by disco dancing until 2 a.m. – all for £1.70 admission and around £3 for a drink.

You can also gamble in the casinos and go to opera, ballet and symphony concerts in splendid settings, both in Cannes and nearby Nice.

And when the winter sun comes up next day? The attractions are almost limitless: you can go to the races, fish for mullet, windsurf, play tennis and golf, hire a horse to ride, swim in a heated pool, join an excursion to the ski slopes or across the Italian border. You can tour the Riviera at your own pace by hiring a car or in the least expensive way of all: by taking the local buses and trains.

All those glamorous Riviera holiday and beauty spots are within such easy reach: Antibes, St Tropez, Nice and, off the famous corniche road, Villefranche, Monte Carlo, and the Italianate beauty of Menton. The hinterland, too, with its hilltop villages, fabulous views and cosy little restaurants, is a sheer delight.

On my last night in Cannes I dined in style. I chose the opulent setting of a leading hotel and started with rich crab soup and 'floating islands' of shrimps and whipped egg.

For my main course I had a selection of fine Mediterranean fish with croutons in a cream and saffron sauce with vegetables. And I ended with little pancakes flamed in armagnac, filled with praline, sprinkled with almonds and topped with fresh tangerine and grapefruit – fabulous.

With wine, coffee and service, that dinner cost me £14. It was easily the most expensive of my trip, but I had not only superb food in a great setting but entertainment by a trio, including a pretty girl singer, and the chance to dance until the early hours to discs of the guests' choice and played not so loudly as to blast your head off. Played at a volume to suit my mood exactly.

The Croisette was peaceful under the moon when I took my last stroll. Like every other Briton I met, I was full of plans to take glacé fruits and mimosa home with me next day to retain just a little longer the sweet taste and the scent of my Riviera break. But I knew too that my memory of that perfect week would last long after the sweets had been eaten and the flowers had died.

Hotel – Les Alpes.
Meal at Entrevaux – Restaurant Vauban.
Fish meal in Cannes – Restaurant Le Bourgogne.
Dinner at Croisette – L'Assiette au Boeuf.
Expensive dinner and entertainment – Jane's.
Cabaret – Loew's Hotel.

ITALY

12 TUSCANY –
THE TIMELESS CHARM

There was a dream-like quality about that summer night on the lake under the Tuscan moon . . . The Apuan Alps silver-tipped against the stars, the ghostly white gleam of a swan's plumage among the reeds, the scent of pine from the shore, the only sound the gentle splash of the oars as the old boatman rowed me from Massaciuccoli village towards Torre del Lago.

And then came magic of a different sort – an Italian tenor in full voice.

The old man stopped rowing, put a finger to his lips and murmured: '*Fantastico!*' Music swelled as the voice died away.

I looked towards the twinkling lights of Torre del Lago, to the brightest cluster of them at an open-air theatre on the shore, where each summer the finest singers in all Italy pay tribute to Puccini, the maestro who wrote and died in a villa there.

I'm no opera fanatic but you would have to be a philistine and completely tone deaf not to be enchanted by a voice and orchestral music like that in such a setting. The rehearsal was still going on as we landed among the palms and weeping willows on the bank.

And the glorious voices which filled the little restaurant – named, naturally, after a Puccini opera – where I sat down to a dinner, I am sure would have had the approval of Puccini himself. Like all good Tuscans, he loved his food.

Positively tiptoeing so that I would not miss a note of music, the waiter brought me a superb risotto of shrimps, clams and squid, then a succulent veal cooked in cream, wine and mushrooms and accompanied by a crisp salad and fresh crusty bread. For dessert I had Tuscany's favourite sweet dish: zuccotto, a rich concoction of soufflé glacé, light sponge, chocolate, and almond liqueur. With coffee and a half-bottle of Tuscan wine, dinner in that romantic spot cost me £8.50.

The old cathedral in Siena

I lingered over it, looking out on the moonlit water, listening to *Turandot* and reflecting what magnificent contrasts there are to delight a visitor to this corner of north-west Italy.

Torre del Lago is a resort with a touch of sophistication. My trip with the boatman had returned me from a different world. Massaciuccoli, which gives the lake its name, is simplicity itself:

a Tuscan village of ancient rambling houses lining narrow streets, nestling in vineyards, orange and lemon groves, hydrangeas, carnations and roses.

Now I had a drive of only three miles through scented avenues of pines and lime trees to yet another Tuscan world: to the bright lights of Viareggio, leading resort of the Versilia Riviera, where the lamps of night fishermen bobbed on the Tyrrhenian Sea lapping wide sandy beaches. Tourists danced on the long promenade to a little orchestra playing among the palms, and cafes were serving the creamiest of cappuccino, delicious chestnut and almond cakes and some of the best ice cream in Italy.

The sands stretch for mile after mile from Viareggio through Lido di Camaiore, Marina di Pietrasanta and Forte dei Marmi. The seafood restaurants are fine, the nightlife varied. You can fish, sail, water-ski, windsurf, play golf, tennis and ride a horse. There are charming old towns to visit: Camaiore and Pietrasanta have old quarters just off the shore so Italian, so romantic and so timeless that they could be a million miles from the twentieth-century holiday scene beside the sea.

You can take boat trips along the coast to beauty spots, join excursions to the great cities of Pisa and Florence, Siena and Lucca with its pink ramparts topped with plane trees, and the island of Elba. You can walk through the magnolia-scented air in the Versailles-like gardens of ancient palaces. The marble Michelangelo chose for his masterpieces gleams in the famous quarries at Carrara – another favourite outing spot.

In the mountains, villages seem to cling to the slopes, sunlight filters through immense chestnut forests, cypresses – symbol of Tuscany – stand like slender, dark uniformed sentries, and rivers tumble dramatically through the heart of deep valleys. The peaches they grow at the foot of the Apuans and the honey produced in almost every little village have all the sweetness of Tuscany itself . . .

You can take home Tuscany fruit as a permanent souvenir – fruit so life-like that your fingers itch to peel the tangerines and peaches, the pears and bananas you buy from roadside kiosks at Carrara. But they are the products of the marble quarries.

This is far from being the least expensive part of Italy. Dinner, bed and breakfast in a small pension costs from £16 a day in July and August, although September prices are lower. Well-equipped camping sites are around £12.50 a day for a family of four with a caravan.

If you prefer a package deal reckon from around £400 in high season for two weeks by the sea with halfboard and flight and slightly less for a self-catering holiday in a country apartment with flight and car hire. But if you bring your own car on a deal of this sort instead of flying, you'll pay around half the price.

You can also take a fly-drive package costing £200 for a week, but this does not include accommodation.

Eating out on the coast can be costly too. But if you choose carefully, you need spend little more than I paid for that delightful lakeside meal and you'll eat real Tuscan food rather than international hotel fare.

My own favourite dining-out spot in Viareggio was tucked away in a quiet street off the promenade. I paid £9 including tip and a half-bottle of house wine to eat in cosy candlelight. I began with some of the best home-made pasta of my trip: *penne all' arrabbiata* in a sauce of peppers, tomatoes and herbs. My main course was a superb sea bass garnished with lemon and served with salad and for dessert I chose a splendid tart of chocolate, nuts, cream, nougat and biscuit.

But I enjoyed still more – and for nearly £1 less – a simple but satisfying Tuscan country meal in the village of Valdicastello. I sat beneath the vines, palms and orange trees of a garden terrace outside an old tapestry-hung villa, converted into a charming restaurant.

A mountain stream bubbled at the foot of the slope; the olive trees stretched into the high distance. I began with fine local ham, served with red peppers and zucchini. Then came mushroom pasta: followed by tender spring chicken cooked with wine, tomatoes and olives and served with salad and mixed hot vegetables. I ended with a light caramel pudding and the price included coffee and a half-litre of local wine.

The next day I would be far away from such rural simplicity; I would walk across the famous Ponte Vecchio and be awed by the masterpieces in the great Florentine galleries.

Florence put me in a perfect mood to spend my last Tuscan evening by the lake at Torre del Lago. The owner of the restaurant I had chosen at the end of my boat trip greeted me like an old friend. 'Ah, the signore comes because he loves opera. The maestro has conquered again,' he said.

'I'm here because I love Tuscany,' I told him.

He beamed. '*Bravissimo signore*,' he said. 'But your Puccini and our Toscana – they are one and the same.'

Listening to the voices and the music from the lake shore under the moon I just had to agree.

Lake dinner – Ristorante Madam Butterfly.
Meal at Viareggio – Trattoria Rugantino.
Mountain meal – Ristorante Wagener.

13 SOUTH TYROL –
ITALY WITH A DIFFERENCE

There could not be a more romantic way to end a day of Alpine splendour.

As the mountain they call the Garden of Roses turned from silver in the full rays of the sun to deep pink, I walked beneath a canopy of vines to dine in a battlemented castle.

In the courtyard bright with flowers, where once armoured knights prepared for battle and huntsmen set out for the chase, a pianist played a melody from a Strauss operetta – a serenade to accompany my aperitif.

Dinner, served in the vaulted castle hall, represented two distinct styles of cooking. For I was in an Alpine region very different from any other.

First they served me the local cured ham of the mountains with horse radish and fresh crisp brown rolls studded with carroway seeds.

Then came *gnocchetti*, a dish of tiny dumpling-like pasta with cream and spinach. My main course was veal steak garnished with cheese, tomatoes, oregano and anchovies and accompanied by a big mixed salad.

And for dessert I had about the best *apfelstrudel* I have eaten outside Vienna. With coffee and a half-bottle of wine my dinner cost me a fraction over £6.

But fine as the meal was, I could not resist the temptation to leave the table between courses and slip outside to watch the nightly miracle of the Rosengarten mountain – the great colour display it presents as evening turns into night. From pink it turned red, then softened into purple under the summer stars when the sun had vanished.

By morning it would be silver again – shining as only the Dolomites can shine beneath a cloudless sky . . .

The people of Bolzano, handsome arcaded capital of the south Tyrol, watch the colour change on the face of the Rosengarten with as much delight as the tourists. Their pride in it is boundless. They are proud of their land, too. And with reason. It is one of the most beautiful regions in all Europe.

But what makes the south Tyrol so different is that the Rosengarten and so many other Dolomite peaks, silvered by the sun, lie in Italy.

Despite all the Alpine-style buildings and the German you hear spoken everywhere, the south Tyrol has been firmly in Italy since the end of the First World War.

It has a special magic, this bilingual holiday land, fifty-six miles long by about 100 wide at the end of the Brenner Pass and bordering Austria and Switzerland.

It has everything – the prettiest towns and villages in all the Alps, and rushing rivers for canoeists and trout fishermen. There are chairlifts, cable cars and winding roads with fabulous views.

There is a long lazy summer with the temperature rising into the eighties and the autumn is splendidly colourful. You'll never see lovelier lakes anywhere in the Alps. You can windsurf, sail and swim. Add to all this that fine combination of all that is best in Austrian and Italian *cuisine* and quite outstanding local wine.

East of Bolzano is one of the loveliest spots of all – the rolling velvety green plateau, 6,000 feet high, of the Seiser Alm, where the views of the surrounding peaks are a joy. There are hotels and pensions on that plateau. You can reach it by cable car from the Gardena Valley or simple drive up.

At the foot of the mountains and above the pretty little town of Seis itself is a pension run by a cheerful blue-eyed Tyrolean lady who ushers her guests into rooms bright with flowers.

The view from the balconies alone is worth the £15 she charges in high season for dinner, bed and breakfast.

I lunched there one day – the little place has a restaurant for passing travellers.

She did me proud, too. For £3.70 – the price included coffee and a jug of wine – she bought me a rich vegetable broth, then pork in a creamy sauce, basil, carrots, and onions, salad, and that

most Austrian of desserts, *kaiserschmarren* – the sweet omelette loved by old Franz Josef and served with cranberries.

If you prefer to rent an apartment and do your own cooking, you pay from around £50 a week. You can also stay on a camp site – often including a swimming pool – charging a family of four with car and caravan from about £10 a day.

One of the few places where you will find a package tour operating is Merano. Two weeks there on half board costs from just over £400.

It is the most sophisticated resort in the region and, like Bolzano, is an ideal centre for excursions to the beauty spots of three countries.

Merano, complete with palm groves, a river promenade, a view of snow-capped mountains, its orchestra playing Strauss and Waldteufel in the afternoon sun, its horsedrawn carriages for stately rides and its racecourse, is so unmistakably a relic of the old Austro-Hungarian empire that you would be barely surprised if bewhiskered old Franz Josef himself passed you on the promenade.

From Merano, too, you can spend a day summer skiing on a mighty glacier, and return in the evening for a splendid dinner and a glass of traditional grape juice as the orchestra serenades you.

But for me the real charm of the south Tyrol is in the valleys and mountains and little spots like Welschnofen and Tiers: the Gardena region and the towns of Ortisei, Wolkenstein, Kastelruth and Seis.

And for a lake holiday – particularly if you like windsurfing – you could not do better than to stay at Kaltern near the Kattersee.

Reached by cable car from Bolzano is another lovely plateau where a wooden tram rattling away since Hapsburg days takes you through larch glades and across meadows, and there is a pick of pensions and hotels.

In Bolzano itself the restaurants are fine. One in the Via Piave charged me just over £7 for the most elegant meal of my stay. After a light pasta cooked in cream with ham, came venison in red wine with a fruit-filled *vol au vent* and accompanied by salad and mixed vegetables.

The dessert was an Italian-style masterpiece: ice cream laced liberally with cherry brandy, studded with cherries and topped with whipped cream. And the price included coffee and a half-litre of wine.

I remember, too, at the end of the road through the apricot trees of the Vinschgau Valley lunching in an enchanting little walled place called Glurns – population 750 and the smallest town in all Italy.

You can walk through it from gateway to gateway in minutes, with the locals calling '*Gruss Gott*' as you pass them in the cobbled streets. So small in fact that farmers actually live within the walls and lead their cows for milking through the town. But there is nothing small about the portions the main inn serves you.

I lunched heartily there for £5 and later climbed the rough track to Churburg Castle. Across the valley the mighty peak of the Ortler, roof of the South Tyrol, was shrouded in the only cloud in sight.

Inside the castle gleamed the swords, breastplates, helmets, horse armour, and banners of the old nobles. I emerged into the sunshine on the castle heights for a grandee's view of his domain to find the cloud had gone. Now the Ortler stood in all its snow-capped glory against the sky.

And I realized just why the long-dead lords of the castle had been so ready to fight for their land.

Dinner in castle – Schloss Maretsch.
Meal at Glurns – Gasthof Post.
Meal at Kaltern – Seegarten.
Meal in pension – I am not revealing the name of this establishment, as I have allied the meal to accommodation and I chose the pension as typical of many at which to eat and/or stay and it would be unfair to crowd the little place out.

14   SORRENTO, CAPRI –
THE LAZY SOUTH

Astern of my little steamer, the cliffs of Capri were honey-coloured in the mellow sunlight of late afternoon.

And far across the Bay of Naples the only cloud in the sky of a perfect day drifted lazily over the tip of Vesuvius – as light and creamy as the topping of the cappuccino I was sipping.

I had relished every moment of my outing from Sorrento to Capri. I had taken a funicular high above the island's harbour past vineyards and banks of dazzling hydrangeas and oleander, had transferred to a chairlift and walked along pine-topped cliffs to see a Caesar's summer villa with breathtaking views.

I had basked in the beauty of the famous Blue Grotto as a boatman rowed me through and strolled into a colonnaded restaurant garden hung with grapes to lunch with a jug of island wine on a deliciously light pasta in a subtle sauce, a tender veal steak in marsale and the island speciality: rich almond gateau.

Now streaking past my steamer on the return voyage to the mainland across the calm waters of the bay, a hydrofoil threw up a huge cloud of spray. Taking it would have cut my forty-five-minute crossing by nearly half, but I was happy with my steamer.

In Campania, deep in Italy's south, travelling at speed and not lingering over every gorgeous panorama is a positive sin. Even the locals flock out at weekends to admire views they must have seen all their lives.

Back in Sorrento, I climbed the steep, narrow streets from the landing stage. Soon the sun would be gone, the bay would be dotted with the bobbing lamps of the night fishermen, the moon would rise over the lemon and orange groves, and in the piazza lights would twinkle in the trees.

Tonight I would tap my feet to the colourful tarantella as folk

There is nowhere quite like it . . . the romantic little square of Capri

dancers whirled on a tiny nightclub stage, and the warm air of the streets outside would be filled with the music of tambourines, guitars and mandolins – the romance of southern Italy in every throbbing note.

But first I would dine Sorrento-style – in a flower-filled restaurant in the Corso Italia just off the piazza. I began with a big platter of mixed seafood – lemon-garnished squid, octopus, shrimps and clams. My main course was a trio of plump quail, brought sizzling from the charcoal grill and served with mixed vegetables including aubergines filled with buffalo-milk cheese.

And for dessert, I chose a creamy chocolate and fruit gateau flavoured with the local mandarin-orange, lemon and maraschino liqueur. The half-bottle of Campanian wine was a treat in itself. And the price with coffee and service – a fraction over £8.

There is nowhere in all Italy quite like Campania. The sun shines for 14 hours a day, the Tyrrhenian Sea is warm enough for swimming from May to the end of September.

You can sail, water-ski, fish for sole and bream and dive for octopus. You can stay on lovely islands like Ischia and Capri, in a mainland resort like Sorrento or Amalfi or choose smaller spots where you still find the atmosphere of a fishing village.

And you can explore beautiful grottoes, climb Vesuvius, see Pompeii and other famous spots.

Ignore tawdry Naples with its traffic-choked streets. And don't let the stories of earthquake damage and after-effects put you off.

Besides, Naples has never looked better than seen from a distance across the great bay or from the top of Vesuvius.

If you prefer a smaller, quieter version of Sorrento I recommend exquisite little Vico Equense a few miles to the north. From the corniche road you look down on a series of rocky coves, far below dramatic headlands, and with white buildings nestling above the sea.

The sweep of Naples Bay ends in a peninsula pointing towards Capri with Sorrento on the west coast and Positano on the east looking out on to the gulf of Salerno.

And Positano for all its fame has that air of a virtually unspoilt fishing village which has inspired lovers of Italy for generations.

If it is beaches you crave rather than small coves, then stay on the Gulf of Salerno instead of Naples Bay. That romantic corniche road snaking far above the sea and with stupendous vistas around virtually every hairpin bend burrows beyond Positano into a rock tunnel.

You emerge into the sun-filled streets of Amalfi where a fountain plays in the main square, an old castle soars high above and the white, black and gold cathedral throws a cool shadow as the sun reaches its height.

Nearby Ravelio combines the peace of a mountain village with a panorama of the Gulf of Salerno staggering even by Campanian standards.

And as that marvellous corniche road – they call it the Amalfi

Drive – sweeps on towards Salerno there is Minori, a palm-fringed little spot set in a tiny curve of the gulf, and Maiori, where terraced vineyards stretch down the mountains to the edge of town and the broad beach is lapped by what to my eyes are the clearest, most inviting waters of all.

From Vico Equense to Maiori the coast runs for around seventy-five miles – to my mind Italy has nothing more beautiful to offer. And the cost of a holiday there? You'll pay less in many other parts of Italy but if there was ever an Italian holiday worth saving for, then this is it.

For a reasonable hotel with half board reckon on from about £15 a day if you travel independently. For a family of four with a car and caravan daily camp site fees are from roughly £10. For a package deal based on Sorrento, for example, and including air fare and two weeks' half board expect to pay from £270.

Cost of nightlife? In Sorrento it ranges from around £2.70 admission fee and one drink included to watch a show featuring those whirling tanantella dancers to discotheques where the price is less and little bars where you drink for about £1.80 a time and listen to strumming troubadours singing Neapolitan serenades.

Eating out can be expensive, especially if you pick fish in a first-class restaurant. Even without fish my lunch on Capri cost me £10 but the setting and food were superb and in more simple surroundings I could have paid less. Particularly in the larger resorts, you can find pleasant little restaurants offering three courses with wine and coffee from around £6.

Near Pompeii I paid for lunch roughly what I was charged in Capri, but it was because I had chosen fish as the main course – and how delicious that juicy sea bream was.

It followed a dish of gnocchi in a rich tomato and cheese sauce and the fish came served with peperoni salad and broccoli. For dessert I chose another of those inimitable Italian gateaux and the price included coffee and a half-bottle of wine.

That lunch was all the more pleasant for the mandolin serenade which accompanied it and the memory of the awe which sweeps over you when you walk the streets of old Pompeii.

You don't have to be particularly interested in classical antiquities to be fascinated by the thought that the paving stones you tread were there in Christ's day and the chariot grooves are still filled with the volcanic dust which choked this Roman city in AD 79.

The marble shop counters are still in place, the water pipes of Cornish lead look almost intact, the cooking bowls are still in the villa kitchens.

Oblivious of the tourists, archaeologists are still at work. After generations of Pompeii being classed as one of the world's most famous tourist attractions it is still yielding up its secrets.

Vesuvius, the culprit, soars serenely overhead – 'since 1944 as well-behaved as an English gentleman, signore', the guide says. And you know that whatever happens you are going to climb that volcano . . .

A chairlift takes you to the crater and the view from 3,000 feet is fabulous.

But you must also, as I did, drive up that winding road back to the heights of Vesuvius on a clear night when there is not so much as a little cappuccino-topping cloud about. You cannot get further after sunset than the foot of the chairlift, but that is more than high enough for a panorama you will always remember.

Beyond the umbrella pines sweeping down the mountainside and softening the harshness of the lava fields, Naples glows with light. Far across the bay the lights of Sorrento are strung out like necklaces and out to sea, beyond the flicker of the fishermen's lamps, Capri glows beneath the moon.

Down in the pine groves someone is strumming a guitar. And like the Neapolitan lovers who come to stroll among the trees, hand in hand, you feel that on such a perfect Campaniari night there is nowhere else on earth you would rather be.

Lunch on Capri – Ristorante La Sceriffa.
Dinner at Sorrento – Ristorante Parrucchiano.
Dinner in Pompeii – Zi Caterina.

15 WINTER ROME – THE SCENT OF CHESTNUTS ROASTING

My welcome at the hotel was as bright and cheerful as the Roman winter sun which had shone out of a totally cloudless sky from the moment that I had boarded the airport coach to the Eternal City.

'Signore has chosen a lovely weekend to visit us,' the receptionist said. 'Now he should go to the Trevi Fountain and throw in a coin to wish for a happy stay here in Rome.'

I was at that hotel just long enough to book in, to cast an appreciative eye around my comfortable spacious room with private bath attached, a room overlooking a quiet courtyard where the noise of the city traffic did not intrude.

Then I headed out of the Via del Tritone for surely the world's most famous fountain just over 100 yards away to throw in my coin and make a wish as generations of visitors to this fabulous city do almost as a ritual.

And what a magic place Rome is, without the dust and the hassle of summer.

I was one of thousands of winter visitors. For this tourist city par excellence attracts admirers from the world over twelve months of the year. But outside the main tourist season you have the feeling that Rome is there just for your special benefit.

I had come on a package tour – not the cheapest nor the shortest on offer, but in my view it was just plain marvellous value.

For the scheduled flight from London's Heathrow Airport and back, plus four nights with breakfast at a good hotel in the heart of the City of Rome you pay an average of £160, depending on the date of travel.

And that hotel with its plush furniture and its cheerful staff could not have been better placed. The Spanish Steps were

The Eternal City viewed from the River Tiber

scarcely much further away than the Trevi Fountain, the Via
Condotti (the Bond Street of Rome) was close by and from the
nearby bus station I could reach the Coliseum in five minutes.

And I could travel any distance by the bus or Metro routes
for 17p.

If you have never been to Rome before then this is the perfect
introduction to it. And if you have known Rome only during
the tourist season, then winter is the time to take a fresh look at
this enchanting city.

For me it was a truly magical experience, that view from
among the orange trees on the Aventine Hills across the River
Tiber with the domes, the winged chariots, the towers, the
palaces and the graceful bridges pink in the mellow winter
afternoon's sun.

There was even room to sit for a moment by the Spanish

Steps while thousands of starlings swirled overhead and the air was filled with the students' guitars and artists displayed their work.

The scent of creamy cappuccino wafting out of a fashionable red plush and marbled cafe in the Via Condotti beyond the brightness of the winter blooms on sale at the foot of the steps, could not have been more tempting.

And for once there was no queue for the most fascinating view of St Peter's Basilica, through the big keyhole in the gates of the Palace of the Maltese Knights.

You gaze straight down the tree-lined garden and across the River Tiber and there is the famous dome, dead centre, shimmering in the sunshine. And as the evening breeze swept down the famous Seven Hills of Rome, the air was fresh enough to carry the scent of the pine trees.

There were other aromas, too: the chestnuts roasting on the stalls in the gorgeous Piazza Navona, the sweetness of the flowers that were for sale and the waft of the dinner being prepared in hundreds of fine little restaurants.

My first meal was simple, delicious and cooked and served impeccably.

First came a big selection of hors d'oeuvres served with rough bread; buffalo-milk cheese and tomatoes; sheep's cheese wrapped in delicate pastry, artichoke hearts in a piquant sauce, spiced meats, sweetcorn and mixed salads.

Then came a light pasta in a cream sauce with celery.

Next was a main dish consisting of tender chunks of beef in a 'Hunter's Brew' of herbs and cream, and then dessert of a superb light chocolate and almond gateau.

With coffee and a half-litre of local wine, I paid just £8.

You will return home from a Roman weekend with so many memories all revolving around the mixture of simplicity and grandeur. That is the real magic of Rome.

I remember the peace of the Pope's Garden that you glimpse from the windows of the treasure house that they call the Vatican Museum. The long shafts of the setting sun outlining the Swiss Guards.

I remember the blissful ice cream and that unmatchable cappuccino they sell in the Piazza Navona.

I remember the hush that fell on to a softly lit piano bar in the Via Marche when a pianist played Chopin to perfection and the more relaxed atmosphere as a guitarist struck up a Neopolitan love song.

There are a thousand ways in which to enjoy winter Rome; you can play golf, ride a horse, trot through the old streets in a horsedrawn carriage and go to the opera or to the ballet or dance to the early hours in either a discotheque or a nightclub.

You can take trips on the romantic Appian Way and you can walk in the Forum, treading the flagstones that once bore imperial chariots.

Even the longest weekend that you can have in Rome – the one that I chose – gives you barely enough time for a tantalizing glimpse.

But however short your stay in beautiful Rome, leave a few hours for about the most rewarding trip that you can make outside the city itself.

Take a forty-minute bus ride to Tivoli, high in the hills, where Italy's second biggest waterfall thunders nearly 600 feet. The 500 fountains and grottoes in the Gardens of the Villa d'Este, where the mountain streams were harnessed centuries ago on their way on to the River Tiber, have a special charm in the winter.

And the gorgeous halls where the Borgias once prowled have a fascination all of their own when the crowds are thin.

In the old town nestling among the orange and olive groves and the ancient cypresses you eat lunch local-style for just £6 including coffee and wine.

They serve you fine mountain ham wound around stick-like bread, delicious little hot maize cakes, cheese, mushrooms, and sausages; a creamy spinach and spiced meat risotto, a huge local trout grilled with mint and lemon garnish, a selection of fine cheeses. And for dessert cream-topped gateau soaked with rum and vermouth liqueur.

From the terraces of Tivoli you look down the hill and across the rolling plains to the Eternal City dominated by the Dome of St Peter's Basilica on the horizon.

And then you find yourself thinking that if the Caesars had actually gone in for tourism, then they would not have needed legions to conquer the world.

All that I know is, that during my winter weekend Rome certainly conquered me.

Hotel – Marini Strand.
First dinner – Marcello's.
Trastavere dinner – Sabatini's.
Piano bar – George's.
Tivoli lunch – Ristorante Belvedere.
NOTE: Rome restaurants should be booked on arrival at hotel.

16 WINTER IN VENICE – NO GIRL IN MY GONDOLA

Slender black gondolas with silver prows rocked gently in the wake of my motor launch from the airport. Children laughed down from hump-backed bridges, lovers walked hand in hand on the canal sides and towering palaces and fairytale domes soared around me.

Venice, in a soft Friday dusk, was there for me to enjoy for a perfect, long weekend break.

I stepped ashore beside a cosy-looking restaurant and followed the travel-agency courier through a short, narrow street into a courtyard filled with shrubs.

I was just three minutes' walk from the tourists' mecca, St Mark's Square, the heart of one of the most fascinating cities in the world. But in the courtyard there was perfect stillness.

Soon I was looking down on it from my neatly furnished hotel room complete with shower. But I did not look for long. In the sky was a soft glow from the lights of the great square. I had arrived just too late for the magic moment when the lamps came to life.

It was an experience I was to enjoy on following evenings – just one of many delights that awaited me.

Pigeons rose in their hundreds as I joined the tourists drawn the year round to St Mark's. The magnificent façade of the Basilica gleamed golden, the mighty tower, symbol of Venice, rose in its majesty and, under the colonnades, the little cafe orchestras were playing sweet music.

Water buses and gondolas plied the nearby waters of the Grand Canal . . . it felt marvellous to be in Venice.

I had chosen an out-of-season package deal that costs between £133 and £173, depending on the date you travel. It gave me the round trip from London by scheduled flight and three nights' bed and breakfast.

That night, I returned to the little restaurant where I had landed earlier. And there, beneath ancient beams in what was once a nobleman's kitchen, where a huge open fire crackled in the hearth and cast a flickering reflection on cooking pots and ancient weapons, I ordered my first Venetian dinner.

First came the best minestrone with pasta I have eaten anywhere. Then deliciously tender beef in a rich sauce of oregano, peppers and tomatoes served with salad.

And for dessert, in a city famed throughout northern Italy for its superb sweets, I had a fine light cake studded with almonds and glacé fruit. And with coffee and a half-litre of wine I paid just £8.

Then I took an evening stroll through my winter-weekend city. Monday evening, when I would leave for home, seemed then as far away as London itself.

I loved it all – the jewellery, leather and lace shops around the Rialto Bridge, the great churches on their islands glowing with light and seeming to drift like galleons under the stars, the throbbing guitars of troubadors serenading the diners in the restaurants around me and the rows of sharp-prowed boats bobbing at their striped mooring posts.

Under the Rialto Bridge six gondolas poled with skill, swept side by side in a great arc across the waters of the Grand Canal, while their passengers were serenaded with an accordion and a singer of soft ballads.

In minutes, enchanted by it all, I was relaxing on cushions in my very own gondola, lazily letting the sturdy gondolier, named Marco, show me Venice in the best and most romantic of all ways.

It wasn't cheap, that gondola ride. I was doing things the expensive way by having a boat to myself. The fifty-minute trip cost me £15, but the sheer bliss of watching those great palaces drift slowly by, with the soft splash of the pole, mingling with the serenades echoing over the waters while the moon gleamed on the whole gorgeous place was, for me, beyond price.

All that was missing to make my happiness complete was a

fair companion. Gondolas are intended for romance.

Marco – in his winter clothes, instead of the traditional shirt and black trousers he would wear under summer skies – seemed genuinely upset that I didn't have a girl to share the ride.

When I told him I was married, he made me promise to bring my wife next time. 'I will be waiting, Signore,' he called as I stepped ashore.

I found the real Venice with his help – a magic which for all the city's plush night clubs, the casino and discotheques, was born in the distant past and makes Venice a timeless treasure to enjoy.

The lovely old buildings and peaceful canals can capture you as a gentle mist comes in from the Adriatic, seagulls sit sleepily rustling their feathers on the mooring posts and gondolas come out of the haze, their tiny lamps flickering.

A plate of lasagne with a glass of wine in a snack bar followed later by a cappuccino and cake in one of the old cafes – the ones in St Mark's Square are pricey but full of atmosphere – seemed just right to fill a break in sightseeing and window shopping.

The Doges Palace with its splendid painted halls connected by the Bridge of Sighs to the prison where those who offended the Doges of old passed to oblivion, is an awesome place to see.

The golden horses which once adorned the façade of the Basilica loom over you in their special museum. The naval museum shows you elaborate figureheads, galleon models and multi-oared galleys dating from the days when Venice was a powerful republic.

And like thousands of tourists before me I climbed the old clock tower and put my fingers in my ears as two great Moorish figures clanged away on the hour as they have done for centuries.

I enjoyed catching a water bus which puttered past the pink castellated walls of the old naval arsenal into the great lagoon and to the island of Murano, a Venice in miniature, complete with a Grand Canal, yet with the fascinating air of an old-time fishing village.

Murano is famous for glass. In the workrooms I saw experts using the skills gained over a thousand years.

But for sheer gastronomic delight there was nothing to beat dinner close to St Mark's Square. It was far from cheap; I paid over £12 with wine and coffee.

Nowhere had I eaten a pasta to equal the dish of mixed ravioli which followed an appetizing paté. There was pink ravioli filled with fresh salmon and the normal type with scallops and soie. And the whole dish came with a rich sauce of stock, cream, and parmesan cheese.

My main course was tender veal cooked with ham and sage seasoned with pepper and white wine and served with salad. And for dessert there was Venice's favourite sweet, a superb gateau called *Tirami Su* – 'it gives me a kick'.

It was rich with Marsala wine, rum, coffee, chocolate, Savoyard biscuit and a hint of a special cheese in the cream.

On Monday, I took a water bus to St Giorgio's Island and climbed the great tower for the best of all views – the panorama of islands, lagoon, the old city itself, the distant Adriatic, and the majestic backdrop of the Dolomites.

The little island was crowded that day for an exhibition by Canaletto. But even such a master could not capture on canvas the real spirit of the city he loved.

And for me, on a perfect winter day, there was nothing quite so satisfying as the thought that the glorious old place was just a short boat ride away.

Hotel – Do Pozzi.
Friday dinner – Ristorante da Raffaela. Piano bar – Londra Palace Hotel.
Saturday dinner – Panada (must be booked).
Sunday dinner – Murano – Di Frati da Papote.
Monday lunch – Locande Montin.

SWITZERLAND

17   THE VALAIS SUMMER

My walk between the ice walls of the cavern deep beneath the great glacier had been fascinating.

Now it was time to leave the chill and the ghostly blue light behind – the warmth of the Swiss Valais sun was waiting at the end of the tunnel.

And there, as Alpine peaks gleamed in a cloudless sky, was the scene which had so captivated me at the end of my drive up the spectacular road to Gletsch in the far north-east corner of this Swiss canton with a magic all its own.

The glacier, its blue glow standing out against the whiteness of the surrounding snow. The breathtaking panorama of mountain tops. And from beneath the glacier, tumbling and creaming down the slope to form a bright sunlit ribbon in the valley at my feet – the Rhone.

I was standing at the source of one of Europe's most famous waterways, watching the beginning of its journey to the distant Mediterranean. Somewhere far from this spot high in the Alps, it would widen and become slower and more majestic. But up here, its surge was as exhilarating as the mountain air of the Valais.

I took the road down again, following the river. I picnicked beside its waters and simple food – bread, Valais cheese, sausage, a handful of apricots from the orchards of the canton and a bottle of beer – never tasted better to me.

The road led me through some Alpine villages, their balconies beneath pointed roofs bright with flowers, where you can stay in a comfortable guest-house on a perfect Swiss holiday.

Villages like Munster and Fiesch. And from Fiesch a cable car runs to an even mightier glacier: the Eggishorn, longest in Europe.

Later, I found another reason for choosing the Valais – elegance and fine food and wine. I dined beside a willow-fringed lake near Sion, the canton's chief town. While I ate, the summer light faded into evening, lamps began to twinkle among the trees and Sion's twin lofty castles had their majesty enhanced with floodlighting. But the swimmers in the lake would splash happily there until midnight.

Dinner was superb: a feathery *vol au vent* with sweetbreads in a cream sauce came first. Then guinea-fowl cooked to perfection with herbs, mushrooms, mixed vegetables and a crisp tossed green salad.

For dessert I chose a soufflé glacé laced with cointreau and topped with chocolate and fresh fruit. There was a half-bottle of Valais wine and delicious little cookies were served with my coffee.

That meal cost me over £11 (you must pay at least this in a first-class restaurant with wine): but the food and setting made it more than worthwhile.

There are less pricey areas of Switzerland, but none more beautiful and satisfying. If there was ever an Alpine spring, summer or autumn holiday worth saving for, this is it. The Valais is Switzerland at its best: fabulous scenery and food, stylish service and just about everything else to delight you.

There are mountains to climb, scores of pretty villages offering as much pleasure to visit as to stay in. Chairlifts, funicular railways and little red mountain trains take you to the heights for idyllic walks and marvellous panoramas and for summer skiing.

The sun is warm enough for you to strip off thousands of feet high among the peaks and get a glorious tan at the same time. Below you velvety green valleys blue with gentians, where the temperature often soars into the eighties echo to the sound of cow bells.

Sunlight gleams among vineyards and peach orchards, Alpine roses and huge forests of fir and pine.

You can fish for trout, go windsurfing and on Lake Geneva sail and water-ski – for the Valais begins at St Gingolph and Bouveret near the French border on the lake in the north-west. It runs south to the St Bernard Pass into Italy, to the mighty Matterhorn and in the far north-east to the Rhone glacier. You can play golf and tennis, hire a horse to ride, and if you stay in one of the main resorts you can end your day in a nightclub with floorshow.

The Valais has its sophistication: it includes Zermatt at the foot of the Matterhorn and is ideal for summer skiing at nearly 13,000 feet; elegant little Saas Fee and the fashionable resorts of Crans and Montana. From the main resorts you can take guided tours to beauty spots in Switzerland, France and Italy.

You can buy a Valais package deal including air fare from Britain and two weeks on half board in a good hotel from around £270. There are fly-drive deals for two weeks including three nights' bed and breakfast costing each of a family of four about £250 and from £165 a head four can fly to Switzerland and rent a Zermatt flat for a two-week stay.

But the Valais is also ideal for the independent traveller with his own car who stays in a village guest-house from about £11 a day half board or £6 a day bed and breakfast; on a camp site charging four people with car and caravan a daily fee of roughly £4.50 or in an apartment or chalet rented from £100 for two weeks.

If you travel outside July and August you often pay around twenty per cent less for accommodation. You can also buy a tourist card which greatly reduces the cost of travelling around the canton by post-bus and on many railway lines.

Staying in a smaller spot might deprive you of sophisticated entertainment, but to my mind there is nothing to beat the more simple side of Valais life. Even a humble beer or a glass of wine in a village cafe after a glorious day out can taste marvellous. And nightclubs are the same the world over.

There are so many charming places to choose: Les Marrecottes and Salvan in the west; Champex beside a lovely lake; handsome Martigny.

But for my money the villages of the Val d'Anniviers in the

heart of the Valais are outstanding and the scenery around them is gorgeous even by Valais standards. There's little Zinal at the head of the valley and old-world St Luc; Vissoie, guarded by an ancient watch tower, and Chandolin, at 6,500 feet probably the highest parish in all Europe.

And there is the gem of the whole valley, Grimentz. Imagine a cluster of centuries-old wooden houses, their flower-filled balconies seeming to lean towards each other across cobbled, narrow streets where cars are barred. Beyond the village the forests seem to rise sheer up the mountainsides to form a soft green backdrop and the distant peaks ride through the air like great ships when whisps of cloud pass by on the wind.

Imagine, too, a Grimentz inn where, after a day in Valais sunshine you sit watching the flames from an open log fire cast flickering reflections on beams and walls. The fire that crackled there on my visit was not to keep out the chill, for the summer evening was delightfully warm. It had been lit to melt the cheese for the raclette meal three of us had ordered – and raclette is the special dish of the Valais.

It is simple enough; there is almost as much pleasure watching the preparations as there is in eating it. You have appetizers of home-dried and smoked meats and sausage eaten with rough country bread. Then, as your hostess bustles up with individual portions of freshly melted cheese, you pepper them to taste, help yourself to tiny onions and gherkins, and a new potato in its skin from the pot before you and eat the cheese while it is still sizzling.

You go on eating little portions of cheese until you either signal you've had enough – for the number of helpings is prodigious – or the cheese itself has finally gone. You sip a couple of glasses of white Valais wine and you end with a big bowl of the delicious local strawberries and raspberries topped with whipped cream and a cup of the best coffee you'll find anywhere.

Simple – yes. But oh how satisfying. And the cost? For the three of us – raclette is essentially a party meal – it worked out at just over £8 per head.

I remember, too, taking the winding road just short of the

entrance of the St Bernard tunnel leading to Italy, heading to
8,000 feet up the mountainside through wild, lovely scenery to
the famous monastery and then going by chairlift even higher to
see a mighty vista of twenty-seven glaciers and the Alps of
France, Switzerland and Italy with Mont Blanc dominating the
horizon.

I came down to visit the monks' proudest possessions, their
dogs, and discovered that the puppies had an appeal which
would melt any heart. I lunched in the small hotel nearby, yards
from the Italian border. And I paid just over £7 for smooth
terrine; a full-flavoured broth of meat, herbs and pasta; *coq au vin*
with mixed salad and tiny fried potatoes cooked with chives; a
fine *mocha parfait* with whipped cream; beer and coffee.

The dining room was crowded and I shared a table with a
British couple who were arguing themselves out of buying a St
Bernard puppy.

As a non-Swiss you can buy a pup when it is four months old.

'Poor little thing would have to go into quarantine. Yes, and
he wouldn't be so small then, would he? . . . Do you realize just
how much these chaps eat? . . . Where would we put him,
anyway?'

'We must have been mad even to think of it,' the husband told
me. 'We're so practical as a rule. It's this bit of Switzerland, I
think. There must be something in the air. It bewitches you.'

'That makes three of us,' I said.

Dinner near Sion – Les Iles.
Dinner at Grimentz – Hotel Moiry.
Lunch at St Bernard Pass – Hotel du Grand Bernard.

18 GENEVA – MY WINTER CITY ON THE LAKE

I awoke in my cosy little room to the cheerful clatter of crockery and the scent of fresh rolls and incomparable Swiss coffee. From my balcony one of Europe's loveliest lakes shimmered in the early-morning winter sunshine and the snowy peaks of the Jura beyond looked their best against an almost cloudless sky.

I headed for breakfast. It was Saturday, the start of my first full day in Geneva and I wasn't going to waste a minute.

'I'm sorry to say, sir, that it is not quite clear enough for you to see Mont Blanc this morning – you'll have to make do with our Swiss mountains,' my host greeted me.

I told him I would try to enjoy myself just the same. It would not be his fault if I failed to make the most of Geneva on this fine winter weekend. I had arrived at his hotel on the previous afternoon after a ninety-minute flight from London and a short bus ride into the city and across the Rhone, as it creamed out of Geneva's lake.

And as soon as I checked in, he and his attractive young wife, both speaking perfect English, filled me with tips on what to do and see.

Their hotel could not have been better placed. It was yards from the lake, just three minutes' walk from one of the city's best shopping streets and ten minutes from the Montmartre-like picturesque old quarter rising high on its hill.

I had not been quite sure of my choice of Geneva as a winter-break destination.

But the city's fascinating mixture of sophistication and old-world Swiss atmosphere soon charmed away my doubts.

The air was tingling and fresh as the wine from the nearby vineyard, the new snow on the peaks seemed to make the sunshine even brighter and the crispness of the leaves underfoot when I took my first stroll along the quays somehow added to my feeling of well-being.

The £139 package deal I had chosen was wonderful value. For this amount I had the return flight from London, three nights' bed and breakfast and – Geneva was all mine from Friday afternoon until I left for home just after lunch on Monday.

For a few pounds less I could have gone home on Sunday but if ever there was a city which demands at least three nights out of season this is it.

It has parks and gardens which are a pleasure to see even in winter. There is the old city quarter with its steep winding cobbled streets and its squares where they floodlight the fountains and garland them with winter blooms, the splendid shops with some of the world's best chocolates and pastries and museums filled with art treasures.

My first dinner there was in a candlelit restaurant where they served me, delicately flavoured with herbs, the best fondue I have eaten anywhere.

The two glasses of Fendant white wine the waiter recommended proved just right, and to round off the meal I chose soufflé glacé topped with chocolate and laced with orange brandy. My bill with excellent coffee plus a tip for the little group of strolling musicians who entertained with songs in French, German, and Italian came to just under £8.

I loved Saturday, my first full day there. I toured the colourful open-air market where you can buy anything from a cavalier's sword to a rare book.

I relished the stiff climb to the heights of the old quarter where the cathedral dominates the skyline and cannon which once roared defiance in Napoleon's wars still guarded the armoury.

At the old League of Nations building an attendant pointed with a sad smile to showcases where documents proved there had been pleas for an international peace agreement as far back as the fifteenth century.

The Swiss are full of surprises. You think of them as the most peaceful souls on earth. But in an ivy-clad château set in a gorgeous park you learn they were the world's most sought-after mercenaries in bygone centuries. There are relics of Swiss

The picturesque old quarter of Geneva

guards who died protecting the French royal family against the revolutionary mob and they show proudly the splendid uniforms of the papal guards still on duty at the Vatican.

Lunch was in perfect Swiss surroundings on board the old paddle-steamer *Valais* which plied the lake from before the First World War and is now a floating restaurant.

I was served, for a little over £8, a rich vegetable broth followed by quenelles of pike in a wine, tomato and crayfish sauce with salad and savoury rice and for dessert a light apricot apple and walnut flan.

And the price included coffee and two glasses of Perlan – Swiss wine is far from cheap but how satisfying it is.

You sit there overlooking the lake and wonder what you'll do on Saturday night: go to a concert or opera, have a flutter at the casino, enjoy a Paris-type nightclub, dance in a discotheque until the early hours, or just find another little bar to be serenaded over beer or a glass of wine.

Saturday dinner was fine, too, even though it cost me over £10 with wine and coffee. I dined by candlelight and to the music the locals love, ranging from folk songs and ballads in Italian, English, and French to calypso numbers.

The main course was a brace of plump quail in white wine with grapes and mixed vegetables.

On Sunday the skies were so clear that Mont Blanc was there on the horizon in all its splendour and I took a bus along the lake to lunch at Hermance, everyone's idea of a Swiss country village and lingered there watching the winter sunshine mellow until the peaks were a deep rich pink.

I did myself proud for my last Geneva dinner. I chose a typical bistro which served me paté studded with green peppers, venison in red wine with salad and potatoes cooked in cream cheese and onions and, for dessert, an iced gateau topped with glacé fruits and with cassis liqueur poured over it.

I had a third of a litre of Dole wine and the usual fine coffee. It cost me about as much as I paid the previous night, but I enjoyed it too much to mind.

This time the serenade was accordion music. Realizing I was British the troubadour sang 'Auld Lang Syne'.

It certainly reflected my mood – my weekend seemed to have sped by. I raised my glass to him and invited him for a drink. Somehow even in the shadow of Mont Blanc that sentimental Scottish air of friends about to part and taking 'a cup of kindness' seemed just right for the occasion.

Hotel – L'Arbalate.
Saturday lunch – Paddle Steamer *Valais*.
Saturday dinner – La Glycine.
Nightclub – Chez Maxim.
Sunday lunch – Cafe de l'Horloge.
Sunday dinner – Restaurant des Beaux-Artes.
NOTE: all restaurants should be booked in advance.

19 WINTER IN LUCERNE – LOOKING FOR WILLIAM TELL

You don't linger on your hotel balcony when the view greeting you is so magnificent. Imagine a panorama of one of the world's loveliest lakes bright with swans and pink in the sunset.

The snow-capped peaks of the Bernese Oberland rise against a clear autumn sky beyond the shore-side villas and poplar groves and the first lights of evening spring up along the fairytale skyline of old Lucerne at the lake's end.

So on that Friday evening after little more than the time it took me to book in, dump my suitcase and take a delighted look from that balcony I was heading for the nearest bus stop.

Fifteen minutes later I was walking the cobbled streets in the heart of the city that was to give me a Swiss off-season break with a difference.

The heart of Lucerne is the heart of the country itself. For this lovely old place on the shores of the Lake of the Four Cantons is the capital of central Switzerland.

It was beside this lake, centuries ago, that the Swiss first proclaimed their independence and founded their nation: here was the homeland of their folk hero William Tell, the place where legends say he performed his greatest deed of patriotic daring.

The famous fourteenth-century covered wooden bridge, symbol of Lucerne and spanning the river at the end of the lake, was a perch for dozens of gulls settling above the banks of autumn blooms.

Ancient frescoed houses lined pedestrian-only streets, pastries and chocolates were in tempting array in shop windows and a marvellous aroma of coffee filled the air.

You don't know what you're missing if like generations of British visitors you see Lucerne only on a day excursion in summer or use it as a transit point in winter to the ski slopes.

By taking a package deal covering the round trip by air from Gatwick to Berne then rail to Lucerne and three nights' bed and breakfast in a comfortable four-star hotel with private shower, I was about to enjoy the city and its gorgeous surroundings to the full from Friday evening to Monday morning. And I could not help thinking that even had I arrived in mid-winter snow, my pleasure would have been just as great.

It's not the least expensive off-season weekend break available and there are less pricey parts of Europe than Switzerland. But I loved every minute of my trip.

The three-night package costs £142, but if you have four nights to spare you can leave for Lucerne on a Wednesday. You then have the choice of flying from Gatwick for £157, Heathrow for £168 or Manchester for £176.

An extra £5 a night gives you half-board terms at the hotel but however tempting the food is there, eating out in Lucerne is such a joy it would be a positive sin to miss the experience.

Friday dinner by candlelight set the standard for my Swiss weekend. For £10 I had perch from the lake cooked in butter; a Lucerne speciality, *Clugelipastete* – a feathery *vol au vent* of veal, brandied grapes and mushrooms with a sauce of wine, cream and saffron for main course, and a splendid apple and hazelnut concoction topped with whipped cream for dessert. The price included coffee and two glasses of Swiss wine.

Later I joined fellow visitors in a discotheque refreshingly different from any other I know.

The music was soft enough to hear yourself talk, the mood changed at the request of the dancers with the disc jockey happy to put on anything from moderns and Beatles numbers to tangoes and even Strauss waltzes. Admission cost £1.75 and a beer £2.50 and you could dance until the early hours.

On Saturday morning I left the hotel armed with a 96p ticket giving me unlimited travel on the city's buses for two days. But there was such pleasure in walking along the romantic tree-lined quays where children were feeding the swans and venerable paddle steamers were tied up for winter among the sailing dinghies that I barely used it.

Over the lake from my hotel I explored a stately villa set in a gorgeous park. Once it was the home of Wagner and the setting for the one human story told about him.

One Christmas morning he conducted a little orchestra on the staircase in the first performance of his newly compiled *Siegfried Idyll* which was dedicated to his baby son. The music was a birthday surprise for his wife who was awakened by it.

You don't have to be a Wagnerian to be touched by the thought of that scene as you climb the staircase and the sentimental music is played softly in the background.

I toured Europe's largest transport museum which has everything from mail coaches and frail Bleriot-era aircraft to modern jetliners and the Gemini space capsule.

In the heart of the city I walked deep in a grotto where a waterfall splashed down a cliff face into a trout pool and saw the huge poignant Dying Lion monument carved out of the rock to honour the Swiss Guards who died defending the French monarchy when the revolutionaries stormed their palace.

Coffee and pastries in those pleasant cafes proved delicious; my lunch of cheese fondue, cognac soufflé glace and wine and coffee for £7 was just right. Dinner in a cosy low-beamed cellar restaurant was a fine round-off to my Lucerne Saturday.

The bill came to £12.50 but for that I had a pleasant three-course meal with coffee and a half-litre of wine. I could dance to the music of a versatile little group and enjoy a relaxed floorshow.

Early mist on Sunday with the swans gliding through it like pale ghosts gave way to a splendid autumn day.

Mount Rigi was my destination and to reach it I took a steamer trip through ever-changing scenery. We passed wooded islands, tiny alpine houses, foothills dotted with villas and castles and mighty towering cliffs.

They call Rigi the queen of Lucerne's mountains and lunch in a restaurant 4,400 feet above sea level at the end of the mountain railway trip was served with a stupendous panorama to admire.

I saw gleaming lakes, the majesty of the Jungfrau and Eiger, and, on the far horizon, just a glimpse of Mont Blanc, the roof of Europe.

You can combine skiing with your Lucerne weekend if you go well into the winter months. You don't have to ski, however to work up a big appetite for the fine food they serve you high on Rigi – the mountain air is a tonic in itself.

For lunch on that glorious autumn Sunday I chose tender venison in a cream and wine sauce with noodles and chestnuts. For dessert I had ice cream with hot raspberries and blueberries and a topping of whipped cream. With coffee and a couple of glasses of wine I paid £8.

Later, as the sunlight softened with the first hint of evening I took a cable car back to the lakeside.

I would be back in Lucerne to see the lovely old city bathed in soft floodlights under the moon, with the prospects of a final magic evening ahead. The gulls whirling above the steamer were waiting to escort me . . .

Hotel – Seeburg.
Friday dinner – Schiff Hotel.
Friday disco – Hotel Flora.
Saturday lunch – Restaurant Fritschi.
Saturday dinner and cabaret – Hotel Flora.
Sunday mountain lunch – Hotel Rigi Kulm.

GREECE

20 ATHENS – A WINTER BREAK

My Greek day began under cloudless skies with the Acropolis gleaming in early-morning autumn sunshine high above Athens as I left my hotel.

Then the *Flying Dolphin* took over – skimming me at thirty-two knots across the calm waters of the Saronic Gulf, past fishing caiques and luxury yachts and through a pattern of lovely islands with the mountains of the mainland on the horizon.

Flying Dolphin is a sleek blue and yellow hydrofoil. She was taking me on an £12.50 round trip to tiny Spetse, which lies just off the Peloponnese shore . . . And a visit to Spetse, an island of peace under autumn and winter skies, is one of the best of all the excursions you can make when you choose Athens for a week's off-season break.

A horsedrawn carriage took me past white and blue cottages, with clematis, hibiscus, bougainvillaea and oleander growing in tiny gardens and out of the island's main village to groves of pine, eucalyptus and cypresses where the air was filled with the scent of thyme and oregano, and cyclamen made tiny splashes of delicate colour beside the road.

I lunched on the terrace of a tiny seafront taverna which served me a starter of yoghurt and cucumber salad with huge tomatoes and rough bread; a main course of tender swordfish steak baked in a rich broth of onions, herbs, olive oil and white wine; a dessert of juicy oranges and with a half-bottle of wine – all for £4.50.

Then it was back to the bright lights in time for the best part of an Athens day – the time in the early evening when the Greek capital begins to unwind for the evening, as the taverns fill and the bouzouki players strum opening airs in the narrow winding streets of the Plaka below the Acropolis.

I spent the evening in the ideal Athenian way. First, with a taverna dinner, I chose a little place in Zaimi Street and began with the mixed dishes the Greeks love: aubergine salad, squid filled with meat and rice, vine leaves with savoury stuffing and served in a lemon sauce.

For the main dish – tender veal kebab served on the spit wrapped in smoked bacon and cooked with tomatoes and green peppers. For dessert I chose *ekmek* – a delicious eastern sweetmeat of honey, almonds and semolina topped with whipped cream.

And with the coffee and a half-bottle of wine, I was charged, in the heart of a capital city, just £6 – less than a pound more than I paid on Spetse.

After dinner, a show in the Plaka to finish the day. For £4.50, covering admission and a beer, I watched nearly two hours of entertainment – brightly costumed folk dancers whirled, dark-eyed beauties sang love songs and the place went mad with excitement as Zorba's dance was performed in the way it was intended – to the compelling music of a bouzouki, in the hands of an expert.

Yes – it was good to be in Athens in the off-season, without the jostling and the fierce heat of summer. Good to stroll, pleasantly tired, back to my comfortable modern hotel minutes' walk from Constitution Square, the heart of the city.

I had a spacious, comfortable room with shower and balcony. And a week's stay there on bed-and-breakfast terms, arriving on Sunday evening and leaving late the following Sunday afternoon for the airport and the flight of just over three hours back to Luton, proved well worth the package price I paid.

It costs from £107 to £159 depending on the date of travel and it includes a welcome ouzo party at which you are loaded with good advice – where to eat, what to see, the best guided excursions to take.

So close at hand you have two coasts to visit – the city is built on a peninsula. And although the sea will be too cold for

mid-winter swimming, you can often sunbathe at midday and get a tan – for the winter climate can be as good if not better than a fair spring at home.

You do not have to be an ancient-history buff to get a thrill from the Acropolis and the city's fine museums. You can also slip down to the waterfront and bargain with a fisherman to take you out for a day's sport. And you can sail, water-ski and windsurf, as well as play golf and tennis and ride a horse.

Athens has expensive nightlife – dinner, a show and dancing can cost you as much as you would pay in virtually any other Continental capital. But for the price of the best cappuccino outside Rome and a big slice of chocolate gateau that a Viennese

The harbour of Spetse . . . an island of peace

chef would be proud to own, you will enjoy Constitution Square to the full under an Athens moon.

You sit in a cafe, shaded by orange and palm trees. From the square radiate narrow streets lined with shops selling delicate jewellery and curios.

Yards from the magnificent facade of the former royal palace someone is selling freshly caught sponges – for all the world as though you are on the waterfront of a distant, unsophisticated island.

Go to that square on Sunday morning and watch the kilted Evzones changing guard outside the palace – a superb sight.

Away from the square prices are cheaper – you will pay 30p

for an ouzo or Greek brandy in a cafe or 35p for a bottle of beer. You can dance to the early hours in a little club where your first drink is £3 and later ones come cheaper.

A bus takes you any distance in the city for just 10p. And there's a choice of friendly little tavernas charging no more for a good meal with wine than the place which so pleased me on my return from Spetse.

In February and March snow might still cover the mountain-tops but close to the city the almond trees will suddenly burst into full blossom and mimosa will scent the air. Take a picnic to the beach – bread, cheese, salami, olives, oranges and a half-bottle of wine will cost you about £2.

Of all the guided tours on offer none to my mind equals the 220-mile round trip to Delphi. The Ancient Greeks and all their works can be as remote to you as the man on the moon. But if you spend £21 for a day, including lunch, when you follow the route the Greeks took so long ago to consult the Oracle about everything from foreign invasion to a domestic crisis, you will be as fascinated as I was.

From the cotton fields of the Attica plain you climb the lower slopes of Mount Parnassus, Greece's second highest peak.

You pass almond and vine groves, your coach shares the road with goatherds and sheep minders and their flocks, with sturdy old men astride mules and donkeys while villages sit under the olive trees in squares and wave as you pass.

You take your seat in the old theatre carved out of the mountainside and look at a stupendous vista of heights and valleys. You climb further among the cypress groves and come suddenly to the great stadium where chariots once raced.

You slake your thirst, as the ancients did, in a clear stream that bubbles out of the mountainside on its way to water the ancient trees in Greece's biggest olive grove.

Away from the summer heat nightingales sing during the day here – they call them Apollo's songbirds.

You sip your aperitif on a hotel roof and see the sun gleaming on the sea at the foot of the tree-covered slopes. You eat mixed hors d'oeuvres followed by casseroled lamb and fresh fruit.

And perhaps you will be as lucky as I was and see high above you two mighty golden eagles sweeping past Mount Parnassus.

According to Greek legend Zeus determined the centre of the world by releasing two eagles in opposite directions. They met at Delphi . . .

You have over 100 miles to travel back to the big city. But I am willing to bet that if you see those golden eagles you will feel as I did – that they and the beauty around them are as much a part of an Athens holiday as the Acropolis and the bright lights of Constitution Square.

Hotel – Athens Centre.
First dinner – Costoyanis Taverna.
Meal on Spetse – Lyrakis Taverna.
Athens entertainment – Palia Athina.
Meal at Delphi – Hotel Iniohos.

21 ZANTE AND KEFALONIA – IONIAN GEMS

The man with the rubber dinghy waved – and it was time to go, time to let the warm bright sand of the idyllically beautiful little cove and the sea lapping it caress my feet as reluctantly I left my sunbathing spot to join him.

I scrambled aboard, the dinghy's motor burst into life, the beat of it thrown back from the huge cliffs rearing overhead, shattering the silence I had relished on a long dreamy Greek morning at Keri on the southern tip of the island of Zante.

But for me the magic had begun even before I reached that tiny smooth beach, accessible only from the sea. For the dinghy had taken me deep into caverns with high-vaulted roofs and with shafts of sunlight penetrating to make rocks and water sparkle with every colour of the rainbow.

I had watched the sea at the mouth of those caverns turn from aquamarine to turquoise and to deep blue before the process started all over again with the play of sunlight and shadow.

If you think that the special light and colour they say you find only in Greece is a tourist-industry myth a £7 morning excursion to Cape Keri will prove you wrong in the most delightful way.

It is a trip you must make at the start of the day because only in the morning will you see those fantastic colours at their best. Then, after your swim and sunbathe you chug back across Turtle Bay under cloudless blue Ionian skies more than ready for lunch in a little open-air taverna among the gnarled carob trees on the far shore at Dafni.

The charm of Zante lies in its beauty and its simplicity and the lunch awaiting me under the trees was perfect for the surroundings: refreshing yoghurt and cucumber salad, aubergines, and the traditional Greek salad of sweet onions, black olives, feta cheese and huge tomatoes to accompany the Greek national dish moussaka.

There was feathery home-made apple cake and a big bunch of delicious island grapes as dessert. And with coffee and a half-bottle of wine I paid just £3.50.

You linger over a meal in such a setting and later the little beach nearby proves as tempting as the one you left on the far side of the bay. Then, in the mellowing sunshine of later afternoon you drive the rough winding track up the cliffside and bump your way to Keri again to watch the most glorious sunset you can see anywhere.

Later still, to round off a perfect Zante day, you head back under the rising moon to the island's little capital. And if you feel really romantic you abandon your car for a horsedrawn carriage which takes the colonnaded waterfront to a little seafood restaurant where the freshly caught mullet is as pink as the sunset you admired a short time earlier.

It all added up to a marvellous way of spending my first day on Zante and the best of all proofs that the Ionian Islands lying off the shore of western Greece are not mere outposts of sophisticated Corfu.

Choose Zante and you bask in summer temperatures heading through the eighties, where the sun shines for over twelve hours a day and you can swim from spring to the end of September, where the bougainvillaea is so bright that it dazzles, and the local melons and thyme-flavoured honey are unbeatable.

Zante's old Venetian rulers called the island '*fior di levante*' – flower of the East. And I can't think of a better description.

It is only small – twenty miles long by twelve miles wide – but it packs in so many pleasures that you will never feel bored. You can fish for bass and mullet and dive for octopus and lobster. You can sail, water-ski, windsurf, play tennis. There are guided tours to local beauty spots and to Olympia on the Greek mainland.

And if you bring your car on the ferry, you can camp cheaply, pay £6.50 or so for bed and breakfast in a small hotel or £7.50 a night for a double room in a private house and eat in tavernas charging around £4 for a meal with wine.

For more comfort there are good hotels which cost around £12 a day half board and if you prefer a package deal including air fare and half board, reckon on around £380 for two weeks.

Nightlife is as simple as the place itself: a discotheque or two, a couple of spots where you pay £1.50 for a bottle of wine and listen to bouzoukis and mandolins.

But you don't go to Zante just for nightlife: you go to watch turtles coming up the beach under the stars to lay their eggs in the sand, to eat yoghurt laced with honey, to stroll through sleepy villages where old ladies sit outside cottage doors making delicate lace and to sun yourself on tiny secluded beaches.

It is an island where you share a mountain road with drowsy goats and equally drowsy countrymen on laden donkeys.

If there is an even better way as an independent traveller to have the perfect Ionian holiday it is to divide your stay between Zante and its larger northern neighbour Kefalonia which has a direct ferry connection with the Italian port of Brindisi.

The scenery is more dramatic and hovering eagles uncannily keep pace with you as you take winding roads down mountainsides to lush valleys.

Ithaka, the home of Odysseus, lies just a short boat ride away and makes a first-rate excursion for a day. But you don't have to leave Kefalonia or even Zante to feel yourself in the domain of the most famous Greek hero of them all: he was king of all three islands.

You can take a package holiday on Kefalonia: two weeks' half board costs from £350 in a hotel near the pine-fringed beaches with easy reach of the capital Argostolion. But if you prefer the simple life stay in a small hotel or rent a room in tiny spots which seem a world away from the cheerful bustle of the island's capital.

There is Ephemia on the east coast overlooked by mountains and with a sea of marvellous colours even by Greek standards; Fiskardon in the far north where yachts and cabin cruisers moor beside fishing caiques, and pines and cypresses sweep down the mountainside almost to the edge of the tiny bay with its picturesque waterfront. In Fiskardon just over £5 will buy you a fish meal with salad, wine, coffee and fruit.

There is Scala in the south-east where you step straight from the rustling sweetness of pinewoods on to the beach. And my own favourite, Assos, built on a neck of land on the north-west coast and overlooked by a majestic old castle.

And try the island speciality, pitta pie. It was the main dish on the menu of a restaurant I choose near Argostolion – spiced lamb wrapped in delicate pastry with herbs and rice and served with baby marrows and stuffed aubergines.

With fried seafood as a starter and accompanied by salad, with fresh fruit to finish and including coffee and wine, I paid £7.

Kefalonia is the largest of the Ionian Islands – sixty-two miles long by twenty-eight wide. It is better known on the tourist scene than Zante and there is a much larger range of inclusive holidays. But tourism has no more spoilt its simple charm than it has spoilt Zante's. And to combine both islands on an Ionian holiday is to enhance their magic.

It is a magic which captures you the moment you land and somehow those old Greek myths and legends seem to make sense after all. Certainly my last meal on Zante was fit to have been set before Odysseus himself after he returned in triumph having defeated all his enemies and the temptations of his epic voyage homewards from Troy.

It was served on a terrace overlooking the beach at Laganas, south of Zante town and it was superb. First, they brought me rice and spiced meat wrapped in vine leaves with a lemon sauce; then freshly caught mullet cooked with green peppers and topped with a mayonnaise sauce.

The main course was Zante's speciality, a rich veal goulash with tomatoes and oregano. There was one of those splendid salads and for dessert an intriguing concoction of honey, yoghurt and fresh sliced local peach. And the price with coffee and a half-bottle of wine? Just £8.

What better way to celebrate a homecoming. Odysseus would have loved it.

Lunch after boat trip – At Dafni Camping and Bungalows.
Fish meal at Fiskardon – Taverna E. Fele.
Dinner of island specialities – Restaurant Limanaki.
Dinner at Leganas – Mimosa Beach Hotel.

22   EVIA –
THE FORGOTTEN ISLAND

It was the ideal time to arrive on my Greek holiday island and to feel its charm – a few hours before the start of an early spring festival.

The best of Aegean fish was being carried from bobbing caiques to the waterfront tavernas, bright awnings were being unfurled and tables and chairs dusted and set out in the hope of a warm enough evening for leisurely eating and drinking on the quay of Halkis.

As the moon rose the waterfront would blaze with lights and bouzouki music would set the diners' feet tapping. Evia would be shaking itself awake, from the long months of winter calm.

But the celebrations were a long sun-filled afternoon away – I had crossed from the mainland at midday. The proprietor of the little restaurant I chose was not too busy to break off and give a rare British out-of-season visitor a real Evia welcome.

In Greek style, he took me into his kitchen and showed me the fish in his display cabinet and his big selection of salds, cheeses and fruit. What did I fancy? Everything was fresh and good.

Soon I was sitting contentedly in the Evia sun, tucking into starters of succulent octopus fried with lemon juice followed by rice with herbs wrapped in vine leaves and served in a piquant sauce. The trio of plump red mullet I had chosen came cooked to perfection and accompanied by crusty bread and a huge salad of black olives, sweet onions and tomatoes and feta cheese.

The plate of big local oranges made an ideal dessert, the Greek coffee was as strong and sweet as I could desire and the half-bottle of wine was just right for the occasion. A simple but delicious and very Greek meal – and for £6.50 it was the perfect introduction to Evia.

As I ate I looked out at the scene byond the busy quayside – the great sweep of towering mountains rising to nearly 6,000 feet, the pink and white houses of Halkis, the lofty castle on the cypress-coated hill from where I had enjoyed my first panoramic view of my holiday island.

That castle dominates Halkis, Evia's capital – but, incredibly, it is on the Greek mainland. And Halkis itself is built on both sides of the water. For here, Greece's second largest island – over a hundred miles from north to south and thirty miles wide – is *a mere 150 feet* from the mainland shore and connected by a bridge.

And there is something special about that narrow stretch of the Aegean, too.

A strong current, completely out of keeping with the tideless Mediterranean region, swirls beneath the bridge and mysteriously changes direction up to fourteen times a day.

It has baffled everyone since ancient times, the local at the next table told me proudly. Did I know that Aristotle, who fancied himself as a scientist as well as a philosopher, was so depressed because he could not find a reason for the water's behaviour that he finally committed suicide by jumping in?

What intrigued me about Evia, however, was not that ancient puzzle but the fact that its closeness to the mainland did nothing to dispel the special island atmosphere you feel the moment you cross the bridge at Halkis.

Now if you yearn this spring, summer or autumn for a Greek island holiday and feel it can't be the real thing unless you make a sea crossing you can always arrive after a thirty-minute ferry ride. For the sea widens between island and mainland further along the coast. But crossing that narrow bridge had for me the same effect.

And Halkis is a mere fifty miles from Athens – which means a fast train journey from the mainland shore or about ninety minutes easy driving along the motorway.

The Athenians would be filling those fish tavernas on the waterfront for the first evening of the spring festival. But by the time the moon came up, I would be miles from Halkis, enjoying in a glory of almond blossom the special island world that lies beyond the white houses, the narrow streets, the old Turkish mosque rising from the jasmine, mimosa and palms of the town centre.

Halkis is an excursion spot for Athenians. For a slowly increasing number of British tourists the real charm of Evia is the unspoilt beauty of its mountains, its country air sweet with rosemary and thyme, its lemon, olive and orange groves, dramatic gorges, gleaming sands beneath the headlands of the north coast and the pleasant little beaches fringed by pines and cypresses to the east and south of Halkis.

On this coast, just outside Eretria where the ancients built a temple to Apollo and birds sing in the pines around the gracious old amphitheatre; near the sprawling sleepy fishing village of Amarinthos and at Karistos close to Evia's south-eastern tip, British tourists are finding a Greek island holiday with a charm of its own.

Evia – so new on the organized tourist scene that it probably has fewer overseas visitors per square mile than any other part of Greece – offers virtually every ingredient for a simple holiday in the sun. That sun shines for over twelve hours a day, the thermometer can hit the nineties, the sea is warm enough for swimming from April to October.

There are mountains to climb, bream to catch in clear waters; there is sailing, windsurfing, tennis. Athens is close enough for both organized tours and a day's visit at your own pace – by car,

train or bus. The most famous tourist excursion spots in all
Greece – the Peloponnese and Delphi – are within easy reach,
too.

At the end of a day in the sun you can drink and listen to
bouzouki music and dance under the stars. There are a few
discotheques and occasionally a folk show staged by a leading
hotel. If you want sophistication you must go to Athens – but
who wants sophistication on a Greek holiday island?

Most British tourists take package deals – reckon on an
average of £280 for two weeks with half board and the round air
trip. If you travel independently you can find hotels charging
about £13 a day for half board, camp sites where a family of four
with a caravan pay about £6 a day in fees, and double rooms in
private houses which can be rented for about £7 a night.

Local fish and seafood is splendid. I remember with affection
the squid and full-flavoured bream with salad I was served in a
friendly little place at Amarinthos when the March weather was
so glorious that it would have been a sin to eat indoors. With
coffee, wine and a honey and almond cake called *katafi* lunch
cost me £5.50 – a bargain like everything else on Evia.

But I also remember the succulent scent of the spit-roasted
lamb basted with oregano, which was served one night in a

pine-walled taverna in the village of Gymnou at the foot of the mountains a few miles inland.

There had been a deliciously refreshing starter of mixed yoghurt and cucumber followed by tiny crisp hot cheese cakes. One of those marvellous Greek salads was served with the lamb and there was fresh fruit for dessert. And with coffee and a half-bottle of wine I paid just £4.50.

What an island of simple pleasures this is! I remember the sweetness of the clear mountain stream where I slaked my thirst after a drive to Steni – a sleepy little village near the mouth of a gorge with a river creaming in its heart. And the pleasure of sampling Steni's speciality – yoghurt mixed with honey.

There was the old lady dressed in peasant black dismounting from her donkey to put fresh olive oil in the lamp of a wayside shrine, and the goats and sheep crossing the rough winding road I drove along to Kimi on the far coast north-east of Halkis.

There were the friendly waves of villagers sitting under the olive trees with a solemn beared priest. I remember mountains still with the traces of winter snow on their peaks but lower slopes blue in the spring sun haze, lush valleys filled with vines and fruit trees, the breathtaking view of sea and hills around every bend and villages clinging to the slopes.

The Kimi road runs downhill towards journey's end. You clear the olive groves and the Aegean sparkles beyond the quayside below you. There are ferries waiting to leave for other islands.

But I'll bet that like me you won't be tempted to take them. Not with Evia's magic all around you.

Lunch at Halkis – Taverna Elladion.
Lunch at Amarinthos – Angelo's Place.
Dinner at Gymnou village – Taverna Dionysius.

23 ALEXANDER THE GREAT'S MACEDONIA

The sudden growl of thunder was loud enough to hear even above the roar of Edessa's huge waterfall plunging nearly a thousand feet down the mountainside.

And for the next few minutes a brief summer storm lashed the creaming torrent into greater fury.

My waiter in the restaurant at the top of the fall bustled up with a dish of sizzling moussaka for this hungry British visitor's lunch. He nodded towards Mount Olympus – Greece's highest mountain – and regarded me with mock severity. 'What have you done to upset Zeus?' he demanded.

'Perhaps he heard me praying for you to get a move on,' I told him.

He grinned. 'Maybe his way of telling you all good things are worth waiting for.' Greek waiters are never at a loss for words . . .

I had to agree – that sample of Greece's national dish, rich with aubergines, was about the best I've eaten anywhere. It came with a magnificent salad of sweet onions, red peppers, olives, cucumbers, rice with herbs, wrapped in vine leaves, and served with goats' milk cheese.

With sweet thick coffee, a half-litre of local wine and a dessert of syrup and nuts wrapped in feathery pastry, my lunch cost me a fraction over £4.

As the storm ended the sun re-emerged to shine more brightly than ever and the quick burst of rain enhanced the scent of the roses around me.

It all helped to confirm the feeling since I arrived that Macedonia – for years the Cinderella of the country's holiday regions – has a magic all its own.

Here in the far north of Greece is a land which has just about everything for holiday perfection.

Here in the land of peaches and incomparable honey, mountains soar high over fertile valleys bright with bougain-villaea and oleander.

There are unspoilt sleepy villages, and 600 miles of beach border a sea warm enough for swimming from spring to October. Cypress and pine forests make it greener and fresher to the eye than the south, but the summer temperature heads into the nineties and the sun shines for fourteen hours a day.

It is the land of Alexander the Great, stretching from Mount Olympus in the west to beyond Kavala and the island of Thassos in the east.

There are lovely mountain trout lakes where pelicans preen themselves among the reeds. On rooftops storks dream away the sunny days, seeming to nod in time to the sound of sheep and goat bells; old men doze over their ouzo beneath olive trees shading village streets.

A holiday can be as active or as lazy as you wish. You can sail, water-ski, windsurf, play golf and tennis, climb mountains, explore caverns of bizarre beauty, fish for mullet and bream, dive for crab and octopus, dance to bouzoukis under the stars.

You can stay in or near Salonika, handsome capital of the north and Greece's second city and make trips to spots as appealing as nearby Edessa, to Pella, birthplace of Alexander and Vergina, where much of the golden hoard of the old Macedonian rulers was recently unearthed.

Or you can follow the example of many British visitors and stay on two of the three peninsulas of Halkidiki jutting into the Aegean south-east of Salonika.

The third and easternmost mainland reached by a bridge spanning a canal built five centuries before Christ, is the mysterious closed world of the monks of Mount Athos. It is barred to women, who can only glimpse it from an excursion boat, but men can apply for a special permit and share the lives of the grave bearded monks there for a few days.

The two other peninsulas are as free as the air above them for enjoyment. There is Sithonia, the middle one of the three. And if you are looking for a touch of sophistication you will find it in the swish modern resort of Porto Carras, where they offer everything from the region's only eighteen-hole golf course to a yachting marina and nightclubs.

Dining in Porto Carras at a hotel featured by British tour operators, I was offered a choice of international food or spicier Greek dishes. I chose Greek and was not disappointed.

First came spiced meat wrapped in vine leaves and served in a rich lemon and egg sauce; then lamb Macedonian-style cooked with tomatoes, onions, peppers and laurel leaves and served with one of those splendid Greek salads; and for dessert a concoction of candied fruits whipped with cream and topped with cherries.

But I found even more pleasure eating in simpler surroundings. Many guests at Porto Carras enjoy the little tavernas of Neos Marmaras, a village literally within sight of the resort.

There are small spots like it all along the Macedonian shore. They serve you the freshest of fish with salad and dessert, wine and coffee for around £5.50.

I remember a perfect day on Kassandra, westernmost of the peninsula, in a tiny hamlet called Siviris. Brightly painted boats were drawn on the beach beside a handful of white-walled cottages and the locals were gathered to celebrate a feast day with a leisurely lunch and an impromptu sing-song.

I had starters of yoghurt with cucumber and herbs, and a dish of roes beaten in olive oil. My sea bream was white, firm and full of flavour with a lemon and parsley garnish. The salad was as plentiful and fresh as usual. The cost with wine and coffee for myself and a companion was an incredible £7.50.

Kassandra offers many small, satisfying places, some little more than overgrown fishing villages, in which to stay. There are, for instance, the Fourka and Kalandra districts and the main resort of Kalithea, a lively spot set among hills and near pine-topped cliffs.

On the mainland coast of Macedonia, I also liked Metamorfoses, Nea Kalikatria and lovely old Kavala, where a fine castle dominates a palm-fringed waterfront.

It is one of the most attractive towns in all Greece. And if an island atmosphere is essential to your idea of a real Greek holiday there is idyllic Thassos, lush and green, forty minutes by ferry from the mainland and famous for the gleaming marble the ancients used for their temples.

And the cost of a Macedonian holiday? Most British visitors choose a package deal. A fortnight with half board, including flight, costs from £250; two weeks' half board with flight and hired car included, from around £300 and a fortnight with self-catering accommodation and flight, from £150.

For independent tourists bringing their cars – Salonika is about thirty miles from the Yugoslav border – there are small hotels charging from around £13 a day half board, double rooms in private houses to let for about £7 a day, furnished flats for just over £20 a day and camping for a family with caravan for roughly £6 daily.

But to my mind there is so much about Macedonia beyond price. I remember climbing a hill above Vergina to gaze from the ruins of the old Macedonian rulers' palace there far across the great plain. It was easy to see why, apart from the breathtaking view, they chose to build on that height – the cool breeze which fanned my cheeks always blows there, even on the hottest summer day.

A mile or two away, archaeologists who unearthed the treasures from the tomb of Alexander's father Philip – the dazzling gold diadems and chests, the swords, the bronze helmet and gold-encrusted armour I had seen in the Salonika museum – were still working, still looking for the deep tomb of the mighty warrior who had spread the name of Macedonia throughout the ancient world.

Yet to me, high on that lovely hillside, it seemed as if the greatest treasure Alexander had left behind him was free under the sun for all to enjoy – Macedonia itself.

Lunch at Edessa – Restaurant Katappaktai.
Dinner at Porto Carras – Meliton Hotel.
Lunch at Siviris – Taverna Chrissi Akti.

CYPRUS

24 GREECE WITH A LITTLE BIT OF BRITAIN

I wasn't meaning to eavesdrop, but even the lightest of Mediterranean breezes rustling the mimosas near the hotel pool had died and it was a gloriously peaceful morning at Ayia Napa.

And I paused in my leisurely breakfast of big oranges and freshly baked bread, spread with Cyprus honey, as the sound of voices reached me from below my sun-filled balcony.

'Hailstones . . . must have been the size of coconuts, thumping on the plane roof at Heathrow . . . I couldn't believe how lovely it was to escape when we landed here . . .'

'It's been getting on for seventy all the week . . . not a cloud in the sky. Well, look at us; there's the proof.'

I could not resist peering over the balcony rail. And there they were: two pale newcomers from the chill of Britain and a couple with a tan worthy of a tour operator's brochure.

They were heading for the beach which ran in a dazzling golden curve around the bay. That beach was my morning's destination too. My tan couldn't quite match up yet, but then I had only been on Cyprus two days. The tourist season had barely got under way, but already sails were blossoming off the sands and the first swimmers of the year were splashing in clear waters.

At lunchtime I wandered contentedly down to Ayia Napa village, a pleasant little spot on the island's south-eastern tip where you leave the bustle around the harbour-side tavernas and coffee shops to stroll through the courtyard of a shore-side monastery shaded by a thousand-year-old fig tree.

My lunch on the quayside was just right for the setting: first, mixed hors d'oeuvres Cyprus-style – yoghurt, cucumbers, huge tomatoes, black olives, goats' cheese and 'dips' of creamed roes and sesame eaten with rough country bread.

Then came lightly fried squid garnished with lemon and a · main course of superb sea bass with subtle herbs and spices. For dessert a dish of local fruit. With coffee and a half-bottle of wine my lunch cost £7.50.

Not for the first time since I had arrived on this Common-wealth island at the far eastern end of the Mediterranean I found myself reflecting that it took more than an invasion to spoil the magic of Cyprus.

Forty per cent of the island, including the two leading resorts, was lost when the Turkish army stormed ashore ten years ago. Then the Greek Cypriots were left with just 4,000 beds to offer visitors. Today there are over 15,000 beds in hotels and apartments at Ayia Napa, Limassol and Paphos. And however deep the age-old rift between Turk and Greek, the miracle of Cyprus to my mind is that the pleasure a tourist gets when he chooses the island for a spring, summer or autumn holiday is the same as ever.

But it is so much more than a matter of new hotels and blocks of flats or of the locals putting on a brave face for the benefit of tourists. Cyprus has so much to offer a visitor from Britain seeking the sun and peaceful beauty.

Around the cape north-east of Ayia Napa, for example, you can find lovely little bays at the foot of cliffs, accessible only by the boats you can hire or the craft of local fishermen who will give you a lift there for a day's quiet sunbathing. And the fishermen will take you out for a day's sport.

In the main resorts you can sail, water-ski, windsurf. You can play tennis and golf, ride horses, take trips to beauty spots, explore romantic old temples and castles and head high into the mountains to fish for trout.

The timeless Cyprus charm captures you with bright bougainvillaea and hibiscus, with orange and lemon groves, vineyards, and villages where women sun themselves at cottage doorways making delicate lace. And the relics of British rule live on: driving on the left, and English being the second language.

Combine it all with a marvellous climate: thirteen hours of sunshine a day, temperatures soaring into the nineties and the place is irresistible.

Most British visitors choose a package tour including flight: two weeks with half board cost from about £400 and a place in a family-sized apartment from just over £300. You can also take a fly-drive package.

If you prefer to travel independently you can find hotels charging from about £12 a day for half board, and if you bring your caravan or tent on the ferries from Italy or Greece, you can stay on well-equipped camp sites charging roughly £4 a day for a family of four. Hotels make reductions for children sharing their parents' rooms and babysitters are easy to come by.

Where to stay? Apart from appealing little Ayia Napa, there's Paphos with its fishing-village atmosphere and Limassol, the largest resort and with the liveliest and most varied nightlife on the island.

There I enjoyed a night out in a taverna, Cyprus-style. My dinner began with those delicious mixed hors d'oeuvres and mixed salads, followed by moussaka, a main course of mixed pork, lamb, liver and chicken kebabs and for dessert a splendid honey and nut gateau called *siamali*. And the cost including coffee and a half-bottle of wine? Just £8.50 . . .

I loved, too, the freedom of the winding mountain roads. There is the sheer delight of the view above the pine trees from the roof of the island, Mount Olympus.

And leaving behind the gorges, waterfalls and fertile valleys and heading back to the sea there is the peace of the old Greek amphitheatre at Curium where the sound of goat bells and birdsong lulls you on a warm afternoon.

There are the cool echoing halls of the Crusaders' Kolossi Castle where the first British tourist of all, Richard the Lion Heart, married his Berengaria on his way to the Holy Land. And the Baths of Aphrodite where a mountain stream cascades down the rocks to form a crystal-clear pool.

Bathe in the pool, they say, and you will feel ten years younger. The influence of the Goddess of Love who, according to Greek mythology, rose from the foam near Paphos, is all-pervading.

You will eat some of the best fruit anywhere in the Mediterranean water melons and strawberries are first-rate. And I hope that if you find yourself at Paphos early one morning you will sip coffee as I did at a tiny quayside cafe below old castle walls and watch the night fishermen come in with their catch and later you will lunch off fine swordfish served on a spit.

My last glimpse of the foursome I had overheard from my hotel balcony at Ayia Napa was on my final day in Cyprus. The lamb they were soon to eat was turning on the spit over a charcoal fire at lofty Platres, more than five thousand feet above the sea.

It was lunchtime, but Cypriots don't wait for night to dance. Suddenly bouzouki music filled the little place and the proprietor and his friends invited everyone to join in Zorba's dance. I've never seen happier, more carefree tourists anywhere.

Lunch at Ayia Napa – Vasos Taverna.
Dinner at Limassol (including entertainment) – Koutouki Taverna.
Lunch at Platres – Aphrodite's Chalet.

HOLLAND

25   ACROSS THE DYKE
TO FRIESLAND

For mile after mile I had driven along the top of the great dyke
dividing two seas, my only company the screaming gulls
whirling above my car and spring lambs frolicking on the green
verges.

Behind me the coast I had left faded over the horizon and
ahead the road seemed to point straight to an empty skyline.

Then, after the further shore appeared in the distance, I saw a
spot of bright colours – a fluttering of red, white and blue flags.
Not the Dutch tricolor I had passed so often on my morning's
easy drive on fine roads from the North Sea ferry at the Hook,
but the white and blue stripes and waterlilies of Friesland.

On this gusty early-spring day high on the twenty-mile dyke
dividing the North Sea and the great lake the Dutch call the
Ijsselmeer – once the Zuider Zee – I had almost reached the end
of the road so few British visitors to Holland think of taking.

The dyke road was behind me now and I found myself in the
salty air of a landscape which would have inspired one of the
Dutch masters' paintings.

All the charms you associate with Holland were there – the
canals complete with gliding swans, the lush meadows with
resting seagulls, the windmills, the comfortable-looking old
farmhouses and thatched barns, the cobbled village streets and
quaysides lined by tall gabled houses, their windows filled with
blooms and looking out on a forest of gently bobbing masts.

But Friesland, the big Dutch province in the north-east of the
country, is not just another bit of Holland – and the Dutch

themselves are the first to say so. The Friesians themselves have their own language and so far as the rest of the Dutch are concerned it might as well be Swahili.

And the locals who insist that their road signs are in both languages will tell you that they are Friesians first and Dutchmen second, and wherever you see the Dutch tricolor there will be the waterlily flag to balance it.

They even have their own 'passports' for visitors. I bought one at the tourist office in old Harlingen. It cost me just under £2 and it gave me nearly £10-worth of reductions in the price of sightseeing, admission to museums and other attractions.

'If you're thinking of coming back in summer,' the official who stamped it told me solemnly, 'don't leave booking till the last moment – we think the Dutch might discover us this year.'

It was not long before I realized just what Friesland had to offer. Delights include some of the most charming old towns in the Netherlands, that timeless landscape, beech forests ideal for picnics, over 3,400 miles of waterways with the best boating and water-sports facilities in all northern Europe, and a string of attractive islands just off the North Sea coast with some of the finest sandy beaches outside the Caribbean and North Africa.

The Friesians call their islands 'the overseas territories' and if Mediterranean warmth is not essential for your seaside holiday they are perfection. But if you are a sailing enthusiast stay on the mainland where thirty reed-bordered lakes, the largest nearly ten miles long, are connected by canals that pass through the prettiest parts of the province.

You can hire yachts and cabin cruisers, you can windsurf, fish for pike and perch, or join fishing parties in the North Sea. There is tennis, golf and riding.

And there is marvellous food, too. On my first evening in Friesland I sat in the old weigh house in the handsome capital Leeuwarden and watched the candlelight flickering on sixteenth-century beams.

Once, the farmers of Friesland brought their butter and cheese by barge to the weigh house, passing under the hump-backed bridges of the canal in the market square outside. But today the old place is a restaurant and the meal was delicious.

First, cheese and onion soup. The main course was tender chunks of beef cooked with red and green peppers and served with a garnish of pears and with sprouts, cauliflower flavoured with nutmeg, a big mixed salad and small deep-roasted potatoes. And for desert an imaginative concoction of mocca ice cream, advocaat liqueur, cashew and pecan nuts and almonds and whipped cream.

There was a glass of good strong Dutch beer and my Friesian-style coffee was topped with cream and laced with berenburg liqueur made from geneva and mixed herbs.

My final destination that night was one of those comfortable old Friesian farmhouses which offer bed and breakfast for just £5.50 a head and with reductions for children sharing their parents' room.

And the sort of breakfast which awaited me when, awakened by the whirr of my host's tractor, I went downstairs, was a good deal heartier than the usual Continental variety.

His wife served eggs, a variety of mixed cold meats, cheeses and breads. In effortless English she gave me a variety of tips on how best to enjoy Friesland and, by the time I was ready to leave, the morning mists had cleared from the meadows, the sun was breaking through, the black and white cows (one to every head of the population, I learned) looked positively glossy and I felt happier than ever that I had crossed that dyke road.

As well as farmhouses Friesland has small hotels charging from £6.50 a day for bed and breakfast and £10 for half board, camp sites where a family of four with a caravan pay about £6 daily and family-sized flats and bungalows to be rented from about £130 a week.

To hire a yacht with four berths for a week costs about £160, sailing dinghies can be hired for the day for £11.50 and to explore the countryside for a day in the most Dutch way of all you can rent a bicycle for £1.70.

At night you can relax in little discos which, except on the rare occasions when they have a group with singers, charge roughly the same for drinks that you pay in the cosy local pubs – 40p for a beer or a glass of geneva.

Where to stay? Apart from the island resorts there are the

water-sports centres of Sneek, Ijlst and Terhorne, where boats
are drawn up right under cottage windows. There are old-world
country towns like Franeker and Bolsward where the town hall
is like a fairytale castle.

Dokkum has a special charm. On the Ijsselmeer coast I fell for
Hindeloopen with fascinating narrow streets and a harbour
which would have delighted Vermeer himself.

And there is Workum where I lunched magnificently for
£4.75 in a flower-filled hotel restaurant looking out on the
tree-lined main square with its golden-lion decorations.

They served me creamy leek and meat broth, then Friesian-
style chicken with spices and cranberries and accompanied by
salad, beans and roast potatoes and for dessert, ice cream with a
local liqueur made of geneva and raisins. And the price included
beer and coffee.

Friesland is full of surprises. I remember being touched by the
tiny museum at Moddergat, a mere huddle of old fishermen's
houses sheltered by the North Sea dyke.

It was filled with beautifully preserved local costumes of the
late nineteenth century, cast off by the locals when a storm
drowned nearly every local fisherman.

For generations they wore mourning black until their grief
was swamped by the national tragedy of the Occupation in the
Second World War.

Today Moddergat is a friendly, smiling, little place and
mourning is a thing of the past.

And in Leeuwarden they have a statue to, of all people, Mata
Hari, shot by the French as a German spy in 1917. In her old
home they have her photographs, table linen, letters and other
mementoes.

The woman who showed me around laughed when I said they
seemed to regard the lady as a heroine. 'Not at all,' she told
me. 'But not wicked either – just daft. And she was a Friesian
after all.'

A more rewarding surprise for me, however, was the tiny
isolated restaurant perched a mile and a half out in the North Sea
at the end of a road on top of a dam where I was to catch a ferry
to Ameland, the main Friesian island.

There I paid £5, including coffee and beer, for a typical starter of pork croquette with mustard sauce, then first-rate plaice cooked to perfection with a garnish of fresh lemon, pickled cucumber, tomatoes, coleslaw, capers and mayonnaise, and for dessert a generous slice of spicy apple cake with whipped cream.

And there was the Piet Hein pancake, fourteen inches wide, named after the Dutch sea hero, which was served to me in the heart of Leeuwarden's old quarter. It was made with onions, paprika, cheese and mushrooms with seafood on the top.

With coffee, a glass of wine and one of those inimitable Dutch ice creams and fruit concoctions it cost me just under £4 and although I was sorry to leave Friesland it sent me on my way feeling good.

And I could not help thinking, as I saw the last waterlily flag fluttering in the breeze from two seas, that even if the locals do regard themselves as Friesians first and Dutchmen second you have not really seen the Netherlands until you have driven that long dyke road.

Meal in weigh house – Herberg de Waag.
Fish meal on dam – Restaurant Land-en Zeezicht.
Pancake meal – 't Pammekoekhuysje.
Meal at Workum – Hotel de Wynburg.

26 ZEELAND – SO CLOSE TO HOME BUT SO DUTCH

The waterfront scene had that so very Dutch early-morning freshness the old masters captured.

The North Sea breeze sent clouds scudding away to reveal the bluest of spring skies.

Shrimp boats rose on the harbour swell. There had been a pre-dawn shower and now the sun sparkled on the rapidly drying cobblestones and the roofs of gabled houses.

Everything looked so clean, so well scrubbed that I could swear the women fish sellers in their full skirts and white bonnets decorated with gold and coral had been up all night making old Vlissingen – Flushing to us – spotless to receive their favourite overseas visitors.

Even the ancient town windmill – the first glimpse you get of Holland as the car ferry from Sheerness ends its seven-hour journey – looked as though it had been polished, sails and all.

I drove down the ramp and to a hotel restaurant for a hearty Dutch breakfast.

And then I headed out of Vlissingen on quiet roads to explore Zeeland, the south-west corner of the Netherlands. It was every Briton's idea of just what Holland should look like: miles of superb dune-fringed beaches, windmills, canals, and villages nestling behind grassy dykes and lovely old towns where the houses had wide windows filled with flowers.

I picnicked beside the lake of Veere, watched wild geese flying in perfect formation and listened to the carillons echoing through the still air from the towers of one of the most beautiful old towns in Holland.

That night I dined in the heart of Middelburg, capital of Zeeland, in an elegant little restaurant.

First they brought me a huge salad of shrimps, mussels and

sole with celery and a mayonnaise and cream sauce. My main dish was Zeeland salmon poached in white wine with peppers, shallots, egg, watercress and lemon and served with mixed vegetables.

For dessert I chose a fine cherry sorbet. And the price including coffee and a carafe of white wine was just £8.30.

I rounded off my first Zeeland day back in Vlissingen, where I was to stay, driving in the moonlight past the statue of the province's greatest hero, stern-faced Admiral de Ruyter – who in his day would not have been so pleased to see British visitors in his native town – to take a nightcap in what was once the local prison tower, now transformed into a comfortable bar below a first-class restaurant.

But salty Vlissingen on Walcheren Island is just one of so many places to stay on a Zeeland holiday. Nearby Middelburg has an elaborate town hall which looks as if it had strayed from a Dutch landscape painting. The narrow streets have shop windows filled with marvellous cakes and pastries.

On the North Sea coast of Walcheren Island, Domburg, snuggling behind its dyke, and Westkapelle have a special old-world charm. On Zuid Beveland I fell for Goes where the streets and harbour are a pleasure to see.

And if you go in summer you can make the most romantic journey of all – a slow stately trip in an elderly sailing barge which links two beautiful towns, Veere on Walcheren and Zierikzee, an Amsterdam in miniature and the gem of the island of Schouwen Duiveland on the north-east end of Holland's longest bridge.

Twenty minutes by car ferry south-east across the Wester-schelde from Vlissingen, you reach the resorts of Dutch Flanders – Cadzand is the most appealing of them.

Why a spring, summer or autumn Zeeland holiday? Not for Mediterranean warmth. The local tourist brochure tells you with endearing frankness: 'We will not try to deceive you – our climate is about the same as yours.'

But if the idea appeals to you of spending a week or two in a romantic timeless old Dutch atmosphere so easy to reach from home on ferry lines to France and Belgium as well as Holland

itself; if you love magnificent food, and huge sandy beaches; and if you fancy a friendly little country where the welcome is the warmest you'll find anywhere on the Continent and where almost everyone speaks English, then Zeeland is ideal.

You can hire a horse to ride, you can fish, go aqualung diving, windsurf, sail and water-ski. You can make coach trips over the Belgian border to Bruges and Brussels, take an easy train journey to The Hague and Amsterdam or simply hire a bicycle Dutch-style and explore Zeeland at your own pace.

How much does a Zeeland holiday cost? You can stay in a pension for as little as £10 a day with half board including a satisfying Dutch breakfast; you can take a double room with breakfast in a private house for £11 for two; rent a furnished flat

or cottage for an average of £110 a week; camp on well-equipped sites charging a family of four with car and caravan just over £6 a day in fees.

Or if you prefer a package deal you can bring your car on the ferry and have a place in a family-sized chalet in a holiday village for a week from £50, or in a hotel from £105.

Zeeland is perfect for family holidays. Hotels offer reduced rates for children sharing parents' rooms and restaurants cook special meals for them. And that big breakfast is so sustaining that what the Dutch call a snack lunch will prove more than sufficient to see you through until evening.

The Dutch idea of a snack is a choice of an immense sweet or savoury pancake a foot wide, an *uitsmijter*, up to *four* eggs on top of roast beef, ham or cheese on bread and followed by the best waffles or the spiciest whipped cream-topped apple cake you've ever eaten.

You can make a fine 'snack' lunch from around £3.50 and for £6 eat a good three-course meal with beer and coffee in a self-service restaurant.

Nightlife? Lots of cosy little bars open to the early hours where a bottle of beer costs 45p, a glass of geneva 40p; discotheques where drinks are slightly pricier and a nightclub or two where for a floor show you pay roughly £3 admission followed by disco prices for your drinks.

But nightclubs and discotheques are the same the world over – you can have a marvellous Zeeland holiday without going within a mile of them. And there is no better way of rounding that holiday off than to dine out in style as I did on my last evening.

The moon was high over Zierikzee, my own favourite Zeeland city complete with old windmill. The golden figure of Neptune above the town hall positively shone.

That meal was the priciest of my trip – ordering a carafe of wine sent the bill to more than £11. But what a dinner it was!

First came a big bowl of Zeeland fish soup laced with white wine, hot with paprika and filled with shrimps, mussels and flounder. There followed the tenderest veal in a cream sauce with mushrooms and served with sprouts, salad and tiny fried potatoes. For dessert I had an exquisite mousse of advocaat liqueur topped with chocolate and whipped cream and with my coffee came delicious little praline cookies.

Perfection, that last candlelit dinner in such a romantic setting. The perfection of Zeeland itself . . . long after the old windmill at Vlissingen had vanished over the horizon I would remember every delicious morsel of it. And there would be so many other delights to remember, too.

Dinner at Middelburg – Restaurant du Theatre.
Dinner in Zierikzee – Restaurant Mondragon.

27   AMSTERDAM – GRANDPA'S CITY

Through the wide windows of my big yellow tram I basked in the charms of one of the world's most beautiful cities, Amsterdam.

Before me were tall, gold-gabled houses with ornate facades and curtains thrown back to show masses of winter blooms, tree-lined canals spanned by hump-backed bridges, fussing glass-topped pleasure boats, floating flower markets, fairytale steeples, and hundreds of cycles parked everywhere.

And whenever the tram rattled to a halt I could hear the sound of my winter-weekend city, too. The harsh cry of seagulls whirling overhead and settling on rooftops and quayposts, the mellow tones of the street organs, the carillons from the lofty church towers.

And everywhere I saw Amsterdam's own flag – red, black and white with three St Andrew's crosses, for all the world like kisses to welcome you.

My Dutch grandfather who, like all born Amsterdammers could down a large salted herring and a class of geneva with practised ease and amazing speed, used to say proudly that there could not be much wrong with a city that bore three kisses on its coat of arms.

Doubtless some heraldic busybody could produce a more pompous explanation for each of those three 'kisses' but grandfather would have preferred his own version and so do I. To me Amsterdam is one big kiss in itself.

Arriving by airport bus at the Dutch capital's central railway station early on a Friday afternoon, after an hour's flight from Gatwick, I had transferred to the tram to reach my hotel. And apart from walking and taking a canal trip, two pleasures still in store for me, there is no better way of seeing Amsterdam. I was almost sorry when the ten-minute ride to Leidseplein, heart of the city's nightlife quarter, came to an end.

My hotel in a quiet tree-lined street nearby was perfectly placed to enable me to enjoy Amsterdam without having to waste valuable time making long trips from one part of the city to the other.

I was just ten minutes' walk from the heart of the capital – Dam Square, with its majestic Royal Palace and the start of the leading pedestrians-only shopping street – the Kalverstraat – and just five minutes from the Leidseplein.

I was paying a package price of £126 for the flight to and from London and two nights in Amsterdam in a comfortable room with private shower and with a big sustaining breakfast, and the price included a number of exciting extras, ranging from a discount for souvenirs to one of Amsterdam's famous canal cruises.

I had the choice of any scheduled service from Gatwick or Heathrow on Friday and Amsterdam was mine to enjoy until I left for home late on Sunday afternoon. I could also have arrived in Amsterdam on Saturday and stayed until Monday. But I'm glad I flew in on a Friday. For I was able to feel the lovely old place begin to relax for the weekend.

Amsterdam in winter has a special atmosphere. When the canal-side elms are bare there is a magic in the air, and when the winter sun breaks through it blows on golden gables and makes even the puddles on the canal banks gleam like Amsterdam diamonds.

I took a canal ride and listened to a witty commentary as we slipped from canals into the busy harbour and back into quieter waters again.

And I watched as the lights of the city sprang up at the end of the afternoon to enhance the old-world atmosphere around me.

With a sharpened appetite I took my seat for the first meal of my weekend in a cosy candlelit bistro in Voorburgwal.

For £7.60 they served me a starter of mussels, followed by a huge beefsteak cooked in madeira with chicken livers and accompanied by a crisp salad and mixed vegetables and, for dessert, ice cream of a creamy richness I swear you will not find

Old Amsterdam . . . a canal trip is fantastic value

anywhere else in Europe. The price included coffee and a glass of good Dutch beer.

I ended my evening in a typical Amsterdam piano bar where you pay 86p for beer while a pianist tinkles lazily through anything from the blues to Frank Sinatra numbers and sings anything that his customers request.

I was up early on a bright crisp Saturday morning, and, armed with a £1.72 ticket giving me a day's unlimited rides on buses and trams, I went off to see some of those famous diamonds being polished by experts.

Do not waste time lingering over lunch – there is so much to see and do. Go to a sandwich bar, take your pick of a variety of fillings for huge crusty rolls – one roll and a bowl of warming pea and meat soup, plus coffee, will cost you less than £1.80.

The Rijksmuseum is irresistible even if you are not art-minded. The centrepiece is Rembrandt's *Nightwatch* – Amsterdam's proudest possession and the work of the city's favourite genius.

And spare some time for the marvellous nautical museum opened recently in the old naval arsenal building overlooking the harbour.

It is crammed with treasures of the East brought home by early explorers, superb models of the ships which once fought us for mastery of the seas, and portraits of the admirals who proved the only match for some of the greatest seamen serving under the British flag.

But do not miss the more simple pleasures of Amsterdam, above all the colourful street markets and those romantic walks along the canals and through quiet courtyards, where the noise of the traffic is suddenly hushed. The lights are twinkling almost before you realize it and it is time for your Saturday night out Amsterdam-style.

For dinner I chose a little place beside one of the most attractive of all the canals and close to Dam Square.

Including coffee and a quarter-litre of wine it cost me over £11, but this was Saturday night, the atmosphere was just right, the service impeccable and the food first-rate.

My starter was herrings in a rich sauce laced with whisky and eaten with hot, crusty bread. My main course was hare cooked in cream and wine and shallots and served with whipped potatoes, red cabbage, apple sauce and cranberries.

And for dessert I picked sorbet with raisins soaked in brandy and with a sauce of advocaat liqueur topped with whipped cream.

The bright lights of the Leidseplein claimed me later. To watch the show at one of Amsterdam's leading nightclubs I paid just over £1 admission and £3 for a beer.

There was dancing until the early hours and the show was

sparkling, lively and professional. The dancers were lithe and attractive, the acrobats suitably daring, and the singers entertained in French and English.

On Sunday morning I took a forty-minute bus ride through the misty Dutch landscape, past windmills and dykes and canals, where swans ruffled their feathers. My destination was Volendam, a pretty fishing village on the shores of the Ijsselmeer, Holland's huge enclosed lake that was once the Zuider Zee. And there I found a timeless world of baggy-trousered fishermen and gently bobbing masts.

Served by a waitress in bright local costume I lunched overlooking a waterfront, lined by trim, painted wooden cottages. And the last meal of my Amsterdam weekend could not have been more Dutch – a starter of full-flavoured local smoked eel, then Volendam plaice in butter, with salad and a selection of hot vegetables, flavoured with nutmeg. To round off the meal I had a generous helping of spicy raisin and apple cake topped with cream.

My bill with coffee and beer came to £9.60. And my only regret was that my stay was coming rapidly to an end . . .

But there were two more pleasures in store. There was still time when I returned to the city for a last, brief stroll along those romantic canals and the view from the big yellow tram taking me back to the station was just as delightful to watch as it had been when I first arrived.

You just don't get tired of looking at Amsterdam.

No wonder grandfather thought the world of it.

Friday dinner – Haesje Claes. This closes early; you must be there by
    6.30 p.m. at the latest.
Friday entertainment – Le Maxim's.
Saturday lunch – Any sandwich bar.
Saturday dinner – Sherrycan.
Saturday nightclub – Blue Note.
Sunday lunch – Hotel/Restaurant Spaander, Volendam.

28 THE HAGUE –
STYLE AND GRACE IN WINTER

The setting could hardly have been more typically Dutch, more *European*. Beyond the wide windows of my restaurant, Scheveningen's huge sandy beach stretched away along the edge of the North Sea to the foot of dunes silvered in winter moonlight. A log fire cast a flickering reflection, vying with the candles in tall silver holders to enrich the glow of the roses on my table.

The last place on earth you would think for the type of meal I was served – twenty-two sizzling dishes set out on rows of tiny heaters filled with choice food from the East, and accompanied by a variety of exotic garnishes and sauces.

There was everything, from shrimp crisps and fried banana to spitted pork in peanut sauce, sweet and sour vegetables, delicious little spicy egg concoctions, tender chunks of meat with subtle flavours, mushrooms and selections of tropical fruits.

But my *rijsstafel*, the magnificent Eastern feast you eat with rice, for all that it is a reminder of the days when Holland ruled distant Indonesia, is as Dutch as those great sand-dunes.

As Dutch as the superb fish lunch served to me in a harbour restaurant earlier that Friday. As Dutch as the very windmills and dykes I had passed on my morning's drive from the ferry terminus at Flushing.

My destination was Scheveningen, the salty old-world town, virtually a suburb of The Hague, where fishermen's wives in shawls, black skirts, elaborate aprons and head-dresses topped with silver and gold chat at the doors of the quayside cottages as their ancestors have done for centuries.

Typically Dutch – and the best of all ways to celebrate as the people of this friendly little country do themselves, the start of the weekend. That feast cost me £9.30 with beer and coffee and

it put me in a perfect mood to enjoy my winter break in Holland
to the full.

I had chosen a package deal for only £60. It included the round
overnight sea trip from Sheerness complete with passage of my
car, outward-bound on Thursday night and returning home
Sunday, two nights in a room with private bath in a first-class
hotel, just five minutes' drive from the sea at Scheveningen and
ten minutes to the centre of The Hague.

And The Hague is the most handsome, gracious old city in all
Holland. They call it the most Dutch city of all.

That hotel provided everything from a big buffet breakfast to
a heated indoor swimming pool and its staff, to whom, like
almost everybody I met, English was simply their second
language, could not have been more helpful with their advice on
what to do and see during my stay.

You can tailor a Dutch winter-weekend break to suit yourself.
You can travel by the day ferry to and from Flushing if you
prefer and also have the choice of spending Saturday and Sunday
nights ashore instead of Friday and Saturday as I did.

You need not even take your car – you can travel by train
from Flushing or the Hook of Holland, terminus of the Harwich
service.

But to my mind, if you miss that drive through the slowly
clearing morning mist across a classical Dutch landscape from
Flushing, you miss so much.

To me it was as much a part of my long weekend's pleasure as
my first glimpse of my destination. With a car, too, you are free
to explore at your own pace some of the lovely old towns
around The Hague.

Holland's seat of government is a delight out of the summer
tourist rush.

It has galleries where the masterpieces of Hals, Rembrandt
and Vermeer glow on the walls, the majestic banner-hung Hall
of Knights where the Dutch Queen opens Parliament, the
elegant Parliament Building itself where swans and herons preen
themselves on a tiny island set in the lake beneath the very
windows, and tall gabled houses worthy of an old master's
canvas.

Picturesque Delft, easily reached from The Hague

And in contrast, there is Scheveningen – half fishing village with a forest of masts bobbing at the quaysides, half sophisticated seaside resort with northern Europe's biggest casino, an indoor swimming pool complete with artificial waves and a lively varied nightlife.

On both my evenings in Holland I chose it as the setting to

enjoy myself after dinner. There you can relax in a candlelit pub, listen to jazz in a club, dance to the early hours in a nightspot below the famous old Kurhaus with its elaborate painted ceiling and huge chandeliers.

Or just be serenaded by a pianist playing romantic numbers in a comfortable bar.

On Saturday night I dined by candlelight in the heart of The Hague, in the gallery of a former warehouse, now a first-rate restaurant. It was easily the most expensive meal of my trip – with coffee and a quarter-litre of wine the bill came to £12.50 – but how delicious and imaginative it was! The starter was avocado mousse with a hint of sherry and thyme and served with a dill and cream sauce.

The main dish was entrecote steak, tender in red wine with mushrooms and served with mixed vegetables and for dessert I picked honey soufflé glacé with blueberries – quite outstanding in my view.

On Sunday I hired a bicycle for £2 and, with the carillons ringing softly through the still air, I rode off along the narrow roads through the dunes and later took my seat before a roaring fire in a little restaurant snuggling among pines and beeches. Then I enjoyed, for my last meal ashore, the sort of pancake only the Dutch can make – large, satisfying and rich with raisins and brandy.

With a bowl of soup as starter and complete with coffee I paid £4 and then, sorry to leave, was back on my bicycle.

I left for home with the feeling that there could be no better way to enjoy Holland and prove at the same time that this splendid little country is so much more than Amsterdam, bulbs and windmills, than by taking a trip to The Hague on a peaceful crisp winter weekend.

Hotel – Bel Air.
Meal at Scheveningen – Lido Restaurant.
Fish meal at Scheveningen – Ducdalf.
Dinner at The Hague – Mangerie.
Lunch at Haarlem – Het Steegje Coffeeshop.

PORTUGAL

29   THE GREEN NORTH –
MINHO AND THE MOUNTAINS

From where I stood high on the sunlit ramparts of Valenca the sound of summer traffic on the frontier bridge I had just crossed was a mere distant hum. For a moment I followed the direction of the old cannon and looked across the river Minho back into Spain.

But from behind me a breeze bore the alluring scent of Portugal – the sweetness of pine mixed with the tang of eucalyptus – and I turned to gaze at wooded mountains rising from a valley filled with vines and bright with flowers.

Minutes later I was walking the narrow, cobbled streets of the most beautiful frontier town in all Europe where the houses are pink and white, their balconies are filled with blooms and the welcome a British visitor receives is as warm as the sun.

Valenca is the best of all introductions to north Portugal. Within its ancient ramparts it seems to combine all the charms of a holiday region thousands of British visitors miss when they fly directly south to Lisbon and the Algarve.

Beyond the walls ox carts creak past ancient windmills as they have for centuries; rivers and lakes sparkle under blue skies; proud castles drowse on hilltops and beside the sands and peaceful dunes which stretch for so much of the seventy-five-mile sweep of Atlantic coast they call the Costa Verde – from the estuary of the River Minho to below Oporto, capital of the north and Portugal's second city.

Inland, handsome old cities wait to be explored. Geres

National Park, a huge area in the far north-east where deer flit through the forest, is a delight in itself.

Apart from the lure of Valenca nothing puts the motorist arriving from the ferry terminals of north Spain in better mood than lunch in the little *pousada* (government inn) set high on the town walls, garden bright with flowers and with a panorama from its dining room as splendid as the one you see from the ramparts.

My lunch that day could not have been more typical. There were starters of spicy sausage, paté, olives, tomatoes and maize bread; a clear, light soup laced with port; grouper fish cooked in a creamy sauce with a touch of mustard and served with red peppers, fresh orange slices and mixed vegetables.

My main course was tender veal sprinkled with lemon juice and accompanied by croquettes rich with herbs and for dessert I had a fine gateau made with honey and flavoured with orange brandy.

And the price with coffee and half a bottle of refreshing and perfectly chilled *vinho verde* from the vineyards close by was just £7.

Relaxed and content after my meal, I drove away between banks of hydrangeas with the happiest of all proofs that in the north you eat better and pay less for the privilege than in virtually any other part of Portugal.

Here you have a choice of a country holiday, a stay by the sea or a combination of both. Virtually every spot you choose on a coast warmed by a summer temperature often in the eighties and with twelve hours' sunshine a day has an individual charm.

South from pretty Caminha is pleasant little Praia de Ancore. There is Viana do Castelo with its fountains, its colonnaded main square filled with flowers and a view from the crest of the hill above which forms the best of all settings for a picnic and lazy day in the sun.

Esposende and Ofir near pinewoods further south have gorgeous sands and dunes.

South of Oporto I also liked stylish Miramar and Aveiro, where beaches gleam both beside the sea and on the edge of a great lagoon.

If you stay on the coast you can take excursions into the countryside. To Barcelos where the markets are filled with Portugal's best pottery; to Braga where a funicular whisks you high above the town to a sunlit lake dazzling with the plumage of swans and doves; to peaceful Amarante and to Guimaraes where one of the most noble of all Portuguese castles towers above you.

If a country-style holiday appeals, you can find small, comfortable hotels charging £8 a day bed and breakfast, and on the coast you pay £10 for the same terms. Camp sites charge a family of four £6 a day. Reckon on about £10 a day for your shopping; with wine as cheap as £1 a bottle you should manage comfortably.

Hotels often have babysitters and there are reduced rates for children sharing their parents' rooms. If you prefer the package deal your flight and two weeks with half board in a resort costs about £300.

But whether you choose a package deal or travel independently north Portugal is a first-rate holiday choice and I think those whose only previous experience of the country has been a package trip to the Algarve might gain the most from it.

It is easy enough by the sea in the height of the season to escape from the crowds – you simply walk along the dunes to a quieter spot. You can play golf, tennis and ride horses. You can sail, fish for bass and mullet and make a private deal with a fisherman to take you out for a day's sport.

The main centres have nightlife: there are a couple of casinos, nightclubs charging about £3 for admission and one drink, discotheques, and lots of friendly little bars where you drink local wine for about 25p a glass.

From the main resorts you can make a trip to Oporto – and Oporto must not be missed. Launches take you down the River Douro under tall graceful bridges past picturesque old buildings which crown the steep riverbanks and houses that seem to climb the slopes. Sailing barges filled with casks of port are tied up to the shore. And on the waterfront simple restaurants offer the most Portuguese of all lunches, for £3 – charcoal-grilled sardines with salad and crusty bread, fruit and a glass of wine.

But for a real night out Oporto-style I recommend a candlelit restaurant set among the old wine lodges beside the river. There, between a marvellous sunset which turned the whole pictures-que city and its river and bridges a deep pink and the appearance of a full moon shining down in full glory, I spent one of the best evenings of my trip. And it cost me just £8.

Dinner began with mixed hors d'oeuvres followed by a seafood rice dish – a cross between Spanish paella and Italian risotto – and cooked with lobster, clams, mussels and shrimps. The main course was a huge beef steak, Portuguese style, topped with egg, and the dessert was a fine almond and cream gateau. The half-bottle of wine recommended was just right.

And the entertainment which ranged from folk dancing and superb guitar playing to a performance by one of the city's leading *fado* singers was just right, too.

I had always thought of *fado* as being soulful stuff, nothing as blood-tingling as flamenco. But that *fado* singer had a lilt in her voice and a sparkle in her eye which somehow transmitted itself even to visitors who could not understand a word of Portu-guese, and I found myself joining enthusiastically in the storm of applause which followed every number.

Oporto's folk hero is our own Duke of Wellington, who ended French domination in the Peninsular War. High on the city's majestic victory column he is the lion in triumph over Napoleon the stricken eagle. But further south, in the old town they call the Portuguese Venice, the locals venerate a far more gentle character than the Iron Duke.

Princess Joana of Portugal, unhappy in love and tired of the gilded luxury of the fifteenth-century royal court, chose to end her days as a nun near the banks of the lagoon at Aveiro. She left to the town not only a lock of her auburn hair, her crucifix and her portrait, but a memory that will never die. For her story has been handed down from generation to generation.

I could see why the Princess chose Aveiro. The very atmosphere breathes peace and old Portuguese romance. I took a motor-launch trip along the palm-fringed canals which lead to the lagoon. In this quiet world of reeds, herons and solemnly flapping pelicans, I transferred to a tiny boat to be poled in narrow channels through a pattern of islands where only the cry of waterfowl broke the silence.

Later I lunched for £6, including wine and coffee, in a *pousada* overlooking the still lagoon waters, watching graceful sailing boats drifting by on their quest for fish.

There was refreshing cold consommé, then the local speciality: cuttlefish cooked in a rich sauce of tomatoes, onions and herbs. Tender pork was brought sizzling from the spit and served on a bed of rice. And for dessert I had a light, creamy cinammon pudding.

It was a meal to linger over in the sunlight of the afternoon with a haze over the waters where the outline of old sailing boats first formed on the horizon and then slowly vanished from sight like a mirage.

For me the enchantment of north Portugal was at its height that day on the lagoon. It was enchantment which captivated me until I drove for the last time through Valenca's narrow gateway and on to the bridge to Spain and home.

Lunches at Aveiro and Valenca – the local *pousada* (Government inn).
Dinner and show at Oporto – Solar das Caves.

30 MADEIRA HAS A LITTLE SISTER – PORTO SANTO

My little plane, taking just twenty minutes to fly between two worlds, swooped low over the sunlit Atlantic and a soaring cliff which gleamed pink in the morning sunshine of a perfect winter day.

Minutes later I was stepping into the warm air of Porto Santo, to discover a lazy, timeless island domain of canvas-sailed windmills, sleepy donkeys and a charm that captured me within minutes.

It was so hard to believe that Madeira, with its lush greenness and subtropical beauty, was in sight on the horizon, dwarfing this tiny spot just nine miles long by four wide. And that such a short time earlier that day I had walked the bustling, handsome avenues of Funchal.

Here there was just the one village – a cluster of white and pink houses nestling among palms with vivid splashes of bougainvillaea.

But if the landscape beyond was not as soothing to the eye as the terraced hills of Madeira, it was easy to see why Madeira people leave their island to the tourists and flock to Porto Santo to relax under the summer sun. For, apart from the peace it offers, Madeira's little sister-island has one glorious asset Madeira lacks: a superb golden beach which runs for nearly six miles along the south coast.

And soon I was basking on those sands in the sunshine which gleams on them for so much of the year, warming the waters which lap them – for Porto Santo has virtually the same climate as Madeira, with temperatures so often well into the seventies and seldom dropping below the sixties.

This was the happiest of all ways to prove that if you have a yen for a Portuguese island holiday with a difference you just cannot do better at virtually any time of year than to divide your break between the two and achieve a perfect combination of simplicity and sophistication.

It is not the least expensive holiday on offer: a fortnight's package tour taking in both islands and complete with half board and the round trip from Britain by air averages just over £450.

You can stay independently on Porto Santo – but because of the distance from Britain and the fact that, as with Madeira itself, there is no way there except by a pricey flight, it is more practical to take a package.

You go to Porto Santo for that marvellous beach, to swim, bargain with a fisherman to take you out for a day's sport, to scuba-dive in clear waters, to windsurf and play tennis. But the most sophisticated way you can spend an evening is to dance in a disco fashioned out of one of those pretty little windmills or watch a weekly folk-dance show and eat spitted chicken with wine and rough bread in a homely little restaurant.

Or to do as I did on my first night there, when the moon rose over that lovely beach and a smiling plump lady who runs a little restaurant just off the sands, cooked me a simple but delicious Porto Santo fish dinner for a mere £4 including a half-bottle of wine.

First she brought me a dish of succulent giant prawns garnished with lemon, then a huge cauldron of grouper and mullet cooked in a rich broth of potatoes, onions, tomatoes and herbs and served with crusty home-made bread.

For dessert I had those full-flavoured little bananas for which the Madeira islands are famous, and with the coffee came her own honey cookies . . .

I took the little plane back to the so-much-better-known of those two worlds, wishing I had arranged to stay longer on Porto Santo. But even in Madeira, for all its reputation for swish hotels, nightlife and elegance, I found an endearing simplicity by going a few miles out of Funchal.

In the fishing village of Camara de Lobos in the shadow of one of the world's highest cliffs, where brightly painted boats cluster in the harbour, women still wash their clothes on the stones in a little stream running to the sea.

I felt the same enchantment at my surroundings as did Sir Winston Churchill so long ago when he painted the village and took tea on a cafe terrace overlooking the cobbled main square with its bandstand. I sat on the terrace in the sunshine to see the view he admired and learnt how the locals still venerate the Great Senhor.

I loved, too, the stupendous mountain scenery you can enjoy on excursions from Funchal. You climb 6,000 feet and, with Funchal looking like a tiny village far below, the clouds suddenly roll away to let in dazzling sunshine.

A world of wheeling hawks and eagles and sure-footed mountain goats, of flower-scented air suddenly tangy with the fragrance of eucalyptus and pine as you climb even higher on winding roads – this is the world of the Madeira uplands.

On Pico do Arieiro – there just can't be a more magnificent spot for a picnic anywhere – you sip *poncha*, the shepherd's fiery tipple distilled from sugar cane, laced with honey and lemon, but you don't need *poncha* to give you a warm glow . . . women making lace outside their cottage doors smile a welcome; you stop to slake your thirst in the sweet pure water tumbling from the rocks.

Back in Funchal, beyond the banana groves, you find most of the hotels and the fine swimming pools. I enjoyed myself as visitors have done for generations. Straw-hatted porters guided my wickerwork toboggan down steep streets in an exhilarating ride and at more stately pace I took a trip in an ox-drawn sledge through palm-fringed avenues.

The markets are a joy to wander through, stacked with avocados, custard apples, passion fruit, guavas and mangoes. And on this island of gorgeous flowers where mimosa blooms the year round and jacaranda bursts out to make a soft blue haze along the avenues under summer skies, there are dazzling arrays of orchids and arum lilies, bird-of-paradise flowers, camellias and poinsettias.

And high over Funchal, among the orange and lemon trees, the wife of Her Brittanic Majesty's consul delights in showing visitors her glasshouses filled with delicate orchids.

There is virtually any sort of watersport you can desire. You can dive for lobster, join deep-sea expeditions for marlin and barracuda, you can play golf and tennis, hire a horse to ride. You can gamble in a plush casino, eat in luxury restaurants, enjoy a Paris-type cabaret.

But you can also find friendly little bars where a glass of wine costs 12p and a bottle of beer 15p. And you don't have to spend the earth to immerse yourself in that special Portuguese atmosphere that a *fado* singer, accompanied by mellow guitars, can create.

I had a splendid evening, *fado* and all, in a little candlelit spot above Funchal, with thousands of lights twinkling on the hillsides around me and the moon gleaming on the distant sea.

Tender beef kebab, its flavour enhanced by subtle herbs and spices, was arranged on tall spits suspended over my table and accompanied by hot crisp cubes of maize, country bread and tomato and onion salad.

My appetite was whetted with an aperitif of chilled Sercial wine and I rounded off my feast with a huge slice of fresh pineapple soaked in Malmsey. And with entertainment, tip, coffee and a jug of wine, I paid just £5.50.

On this lovely island with almost everything to make holiday perfection, a two-week package tour on half board costs around £300 and a place in a family-sized flat about £250.

I say 'almost everything' because the one ingredient missing is a splendid sandy beach. But if that is essential to your holiday, peaceful little Porto Santo is so close at hand.

Madeira and Porto Santo – what a superb combination they make.

Dinner at Porto Santo – Estrela de Calheta.
Dinner in Madeira – Restaurante A-Seta.

31 I LOVE THE AZORES

We had been climbing steadily on the rough winding road from Ponta Delgada. In the breathtaking beauty of the plains the weather could not have been more glorious that April morning; the sun could not have been brighter even in mid-summer.

The azaleas covering the hedges were dazzling. The oxen, taking the strain of the farmers' creaking carts, were down to their summer pace – which meant an even more leisurely progress than usual. And the farmers themselves, dozing over the reins, looked up only to give the car a sleepy wave.

But on the heights of the Caldeira Das Sete Cidades the clouds closed in – reminding me that I was after all in the middle of the Atlantic and it was still only spring.

My drive from the capital of Sao Miguel, largest and most fascinating of the Portuguese Azores, was planned just for one of the world's most romantic vistas: two huge lakes in the heart of a long-extinct volcanic crater – one bright blue, the other green.

Now the mist, damp and clinging, swirled around me but my guide was undismayed. 'One moment, senhor,' she said softly. 'Be patient – and you will see our miracle.'

And what a miracle it was . . . for the clouds began to lift on a refreshing breeze and as they rolled away there was that panorama no glossy photograph could ever reproduce.

Far below me, the green lake and, divided by a bridge, the larger blue one. On either side, the lush green walls of the crater and around those calm waters, a soft velvet landscape of meadows and cedar woods with the white and pink houses of a tiny waterside village standing out in contrast.

The only sound apart from the murmur of the sea beyond the crater was the musical tinkle of cow bells. The only movement – a wheeling Azore hawk, the bird whose name the caravelle crews of long ago gave to the nine islands they found almost halfway between Europe and America.

My guide told me the legend of the two lakes, how they were formed by the tears of a green-eyed shepherd boy and his blue-eyed princess when they were forced to part.

We drove down to the sleepy village of Santa Barbara and a tiny white-walled restaurant decorated with so many azaleas and spring blossoms that it seemed the banks of flowers everywhere had spilled over to fill it with perfume and brightness.

The meal was perfect for the setting – octopus in wine sauce, a mixed dish of pork, beef and chicken cooked slowly over a wood fire with a maize and onion stuffing and accompanied by buttered yams and salad.

There was goats'-milk cheese to follow eaten with hot home-made country bread, and for dessert a salad of the superb island fruit – pineapples, oranges and bananas sprinkled with passion-fruit liqueur. With coffee and a jug of Sao Miguel red wine my lunch cost me £5.50.

The girl who served me had been eight years in the United States. Now she was glad to be home. 'This island is in my bones, in my blood,' she told me. 'I had to come back.'

Sao Miguel – thirty-eight miles long by ten wide – has a charm all its own, a beauty of dramatic headlands with tiny rocky coves ideal for sunbathing in solitude; of small, smooth sandy beaches, of lakes filled with bass, trout and carp, cobbled towns of brightly painted old cottages, ancient windmills nestling in orange and lemon groves, banks of camellias, agapanthas, hibiscus, bougainvillaea, and oleander; tea plantations and tall palms rustling in the breeze from the soft green hills backed by mountains rising to nearly 6,000 feet.

The delight of the place is enhanced in high summer by the misty blue of hydrangeas covering slopes and hedgerows, the sun shines for up to twelve hours a day and the temperature in the high seventies is perfection unless a sizzling heat is essential for your holiday enjoyment.

If you are seeking an island holiday with a difference – here it is. Yes – getting there is expensive. With no charter flights, without even a passenger ferry from Europe, there is no other way there than by scheduled flight from London, changing planes at Lisbon.

Sao Miguel has a handful of hotels – reckon on around £15 a day for half board. You can rent a double room in a private house for roughly £5 a day or take bed-and-breakfast terms in a pension at £8 a day for two.

But with such high air fares it is more practical to buy a package deal. From around £400, including the round flight

from London you can have two weeks in a hotel with bed and breakfast or a place in a family-sized furnished flat. And if that sounds pricey I can only say that Sao Miguel is worth the financial sacrifice.

You can make reasonably priced guided tours to beauty spots, explore lovely grottoes by rowing boat, take a dip in a gently

warm, refreshing mineral lake, swim in sea and lake waters from May to the end of September. You can water-ski, windsurf, play golf and tennis, hire a horse to ride.

A fisherman will take you out in waters rich in mullet, you can dive for octopus and join expeditions to catch barracuda, marlin, swordfish and shark. You can fish for trout, black bass and perch in lake waters.

Ponta Delgada, a charming little town of black and white mosaic pavements, has an elegant arcaded waterfront, and the nearest things to sophisticated eating out you'll find on the island.

Dinner in a leading restaurant there cost me more than than £9 with coffee and wine, but it was a rich experience: creamy fish soup, lobster with paprika, onion and herb dressing, a main course of steak served with salad and fried potatoes – a Sao Miguel steak at its best is unbeatable anywhere in Europe – and for dessert a huge slice of fresh pineapple flamed in rum.

Nightlife? A few bars and discotheques, but you don't go to Sao Miguel for nightlife.

For sheer exoticism the lovely Furnas valley is supreme. The camellias and rhododendrons were at their best on my visit, the azaleas were even more lavish than I had found on my road to the twin lakes. In the middle of them, volcanic springs bubbled. I took a pre-lunch swim in an outdoor pool of steaming mineral waters, then was shown to my table in a restaurant beside one of the loveliest lakes on the island.

First they served me vegetable broth cooked in orthodox fashion.

But there was nothing usual about the way the next dishes were prepared.

I went with my waiter, immaculate in his white tunic, to see for myself. From one steaming volcanic hole in the ground he raked a cloth bag containing my fish cooked with tomatoes and onions; from the other my meat course: veal, pork and chicken with sausage and vegetables cooked slowly in their own juices and absolutely delicious. The bags were loaded on to an ancient wheelbarrow and trundled back to the restaurant.

For dessert I had a light orange and caramel pudding followed by fresh pineapple. With wine and coffee my lunch cost me just £6. Volcanic cooking is no tourist gimmick: the locals in Furnas have used the method for generations. Sao Miguel has no gimmicks. That is one of its greatest charms.

That night, taking off for Lisbon and home I remembered the pretty girl who served me lunch at Santa Barbara and who had forsaken the sophistication of the US to return to her native island dreaming in the middle of the Atlantic.

We had talked of the legend of the lakes formed by lovers' tears and I shall treasure what she said.

'If I didn't think there was something in that story I might not have come back.'

That's Sao Miguel magic for you – powerful enough to leap the ocean.

Lunch at Santa Barbara – Restaurante Cavalo Branco.
Dinner in Ponta Delgada – Restaurante O Coriseo.
Volcanic lunch at Furnas – Hotel Terra Nostra.

SCANDINAVIA

32 NORWAY –
THE MAGNIFICENT FAR NORTH

The American tourist beside me on the catamaran's deck gripped my arm in excitement. 'My God, just look at that!' he shouted. Fascinated, we watched the huge eagle, gleaming gold in the bright sun of the far north, plunging towards its prey.

There was a flurry of foam, the great wings were fully outstretched, and seconds later the eagle was soaring towards its eyrie high in the snow-covered mountains.

'Wild, beautiful and free,' the American murmured. And for me those words were a perfect description of the land we were visiting.

The sun was warm on my face as the catamaran's powerful engines were throttled back to a gentle purr in the narrow entrance to the harbour.

With big ocean gulls whirling around us we glided past a cluster of fishing boats to come alongside a jetty of lashed fir logs. Beyond it lay the village – a group of wooden cabins painted a deep red with little white-framed windows. And beyond the village the mountains rose in majesty.

It was time for another brief stop on the catamaran's regular run from Bodo with passengers and mail for the outlying hamlets and towns set in a pattern of islands and fiords.

The day was so grand, the sky so blue, it was hard to believe that Bodo, the biggest town in a huge region of northern Norway, was a good forty miles inside the Arctic Circle.

Blonde, blue-eyed children and sweatered fishermen waited

to greet us – the whole place seemed to have turned out for the mail boat.

'Are we the only callers today?' I asked our skipper. He grinned. 'Today is Thursday – so there'll be another boat tonight,' he told me. 'Thursday is rush day around here.'

The sun was still bright late that evening, long after the catamaran had returned to Bodo. It filled the little restaurant where I dined at Saltstraumen a few miles from the town and one of the most spectacular beauty spots in all Scandinavia. Here two fiords meet and their waters hurtle through a narrow channel to the sea in a series of foaming whirlpools and eddies.

There were anglers clustering on the shore – they say that even the least experienced cannot fail to make a big catch as fish are thrown to the surface by the sheer force of the waters.

And one of Saltstraumen's finest fish, the local speciality they call *straumkonge* – king of the stream – was on my menu.

My dinner started with a rich full-flavoured fish soup. Then came the *straumkonge*, served with a cream sauce with mixed vegetables and crispbread. And to end my meal were peaches in brandy served with ice cream. There was coffee and a bottle of good strong Norwegian beer.

My dinner in that superb setting cost me £12 – about the least you will pay for a meal with service in a finer restaurant in the north.

'The midnight sun we don't charge for,' the waiter said with a smile as I paid.

In Norway's far north there is no darkness at all in the spring and high-summer months. But only – as I observed from my bedroom window in Bodo that night – a mere softening of the sun towards midnight, allowing you to look straight into it without straining your eyes. By the early hours it was back to full strength again.

That sun can bring summer day temperatures to the high seventies and even more – modest maybe by Mediterranean standards but where else in the world can you find up to twenty-four hours a day sunshine?

And where else, I asked myself so often during my tour, could one find a greater sense of magic and timelessness? For this land

of waterfalls, lakes, mountains, rushing streams and silver birch, is a land of enchantment.

You feel it from the moment on the highway north from the ferry terminus at Bergen when you pass a column surmounted by a metal globe marking the Arctic Circle. For then you know you have left the famous and popular western fiords behind you and are entering a different world.

You can go north by coastal steamer, by train and long-distance bus. But for me there is no better way to relish the vast spaciousness and the peace than by driving in your own car along roads which can be gloriously traffic-free for much of the summer.

Take the road north if you want to fish for trout and salmon, or if you fancy feeling the surge of powerful waters beneath the fragile hull of a canoe. Go north if you love the thought of sailing among deserted islands, bargaining with a fisherman to take you out for a day's sport or to land you on your own island for a day while you picnic and sunbathe far from the crowds.

It will not be the cheapest holiday of your life. For instance beer and wine with your meal can be hair-raisingly expensive. And a twelve-day package holiday in north Norway can cost you £500 or more, whether you travel there by air or sea.

But there is a way of having a holiday in the north of Norway much more cheaply. For instance you can take the North Sea ferry to Bergen with your car – it goes free if there are four passengers – and have free vouchers covering camping costs for a week. The cost for a family of four would be from £310.

You will need two weeks to do the north justice. So you can rent a simple chalet for the entire family on a camp site for about £12 a day.

There are small hotels and pensions offering half board for £15 a day or bed and breakfast from £10, and breakfast is a generous buffet of eggs, cereals, fish, cold meats and mixed breads.

If sea fishing is your idea of bliss, take the steamer to one of the rugged Lofoten islands lying about thirty miles off the coast and connected to each other by bridges and ferries. There you can rent a family-sized cabin built so close to the water that the locals swear you can fish for mackerel, cod and flounder straight out of the windows.

Tour on the mainland, however, and if a brief visit to Tromso, capital of the north, fails to delight you I would be very surprised. The setting is magnificent and if you take the cable car 1,200 feet up the mountain overlooking the town you will see it in full glory.

Tromso lies on an island deep in a fiord with huge snowy peaks dominating the horizon. The pointed roof of the futuristic Arctic Cathedral gleams far below you, the coast steamers, toylike from the heights, cleave their way through calm waters.

I dined in style in Tromso for £14. First I chose a rich broth of tomatoes, onions and cheese. Then a main course of deliciously tender reindeer in cream and wine and served with cranberries, broccoli and a mixed salad. For dessert there was one of the north's most delightful specialities – mountain cloudberries with whipped cream. And the cost included coffee and a bottle of beer.

Further north, the country becomes wilder still and the greater is your feeling that in the vast emptiness civilization is a million miles behind you. The highway leads you to Hammerfest, the world's most northern large town, where reindeer often wander down the main street.

Beyond Hammerfest there is charming little Honningsvag, where brightly painted wooden houses seem to climb the cliff face. You have reached the Arctic now and you bump along the rough street of tiny Skarsvag where the biggest gulls I have ever seen whirl in clouds around the fishing harbour.

A few miles along even rougher roads and you have reached your goal. You stand on the great plateau of the North Cape – the very tip of Europe. A thousand feet below you the waters of the Arctic Ocean cream around the cliff foot. Somewhere over the horizon is the North Pole.

There is no greater sight than the midnight sun watched from the high plateau of the North Cape. But the magic of north Norway will have had you in its spell long before you see its tip.

For me that spell began when I crossed the Arctic Circle and reached its height as I watched the golden eagle swoop down from its mountain eyrie as wild, beautiful and free as the land beneath its great wings.

Fish meal beside whirlpool – Salstraumen Hotel.
Meal in Tromso – Grand Hotel Cafe.

33 WONDER WINTER
IN COPENHAGEN

It was the best, the most romantic of all settings for the start of my winter weekend in Copenhagen. Imagine a square where a fountain plays beside a huge old plane tree – a square lined by tall brightly painted houses which look like a background to a Hans Andersen story.

Dozens of flickering torches set around the edge of the cobblestones give the same warm, glowing welcome that travellers of long ago must have relished on a crisp winter night.

Each of those old buildings – once convents or mansions – is now a fine restaurant.

And in one of them, cosy with candlelight and a crackling log fire, I took my seat for Friday dinner at my hotel near the city centre.

Well before I had reached the torchlit Graabrodretory Square I had come to the conclusion that my winter journey to Copenhagen – it had begun at 2 p.m. the previous day on the ferry from Harwich and ended at 7.15 that Friday evening when I left the boat train at the station near my hotel – was worth all the time and effort.

For the welcome the capital of this pro-British little country gives its out-of-season visitors from across the North Sea and the romantic atmosphere which strikes you as soon as you arrive make an irresistible combination.

Dinner was just fine too. First a big platter of salmon marinated with peppers and topped with fresh cream whipped with horseradish. Then beef cooked with subtle herbs, juicy and delicious in a mustard sauce and served with a huge jacket potato.

There was a fine selection of salad dishes with a variety of dressings on the buffet nearby and the nutty, brown bread was

hot from the oven. And for dessert ice cream flavoured with whisky and rolled in nuts and chocolate ice covered with smooth praline.

My coffee came as it always comes in Denmark – in a large pot left there for me to help myself to as many cups as I liked.

Eating out in a good restaurant can be pricey in Copenhagen – had I ordered wine with my dinner it would have been pricier. As it was that meal with a bottle of Danish beer came to £10.85.

But in such a setting, and with such fine quality and service, I did not feel I was being overcharged.

I had come on a package deal which is excellent value for money. Depending on the date of travel, you pay from £109 to

£127 for a berth on the Thursday-afternoon ferry from Harwich to Esbjerg, the express boat-train journey to Copenhagen, and three nights at a fine hotel just five minutes' walk from the heart of the city and that marvellous shopping area.

The price also covers sightseeing tours and the return journey starting at Copenhagen station late on Monday morning with the ferry landing you back in Britain on Tuesday.

My room at the hotel was typically Scandinavian – light-wood furniture, pastel-shaded decorations, a gleaming private bathroom attached. Breakfast was a big help-yourself buffet of cereals, cheeses, mixed cold meats, breads and feather-light pastries.

And – just as important – a friendly staff with lots of advice on how to make the most of your weekend.

It was the hotel receptionist who suggested the restaurant in the torchlit square on Friday night and who also advised me to sample real Danish atmosphere in a nightspot nearby.

I call it a cross between a beer cellar and a nightclub where you sit at long tables listening to a band with singers slipping effortlessly from Scandinavian folk tunes to modern British, American and French numbers. They played for dancing too.

I paid just over £2 admission and my beer cost me 90p. What I didn't realize at the start was that I was also paying for what you might describe as 'audience participation' for suddenly as the band struck up a local song everyone leapt on to forms and tables, linked hands, danced and sang.

I found myself among them – hauled up on one side by a slim blonde woman and on the other by a large Viking gentleman who hissed in my ear: 'It's a song about feminine beauty.'

They were still celebrating feminine beauty at midnight when my energy gave out and I made for the door.

On Saturday I decided against the organized sightseeing tour and explored on my own. I loved it all – Hans Andersen's old house overlooking a cobbled quay lined by lightships and schooners; the precision of the royal fur-hatted guards marching to a jolly tune called 'George with the Flag' across the octagonal area where four palaces face each other; the pink-faced old ladies with their fish stalls on the waterfront; the morning sun gleaming on the elaborate entwined dragons' tails on the spire of the stock exchange.

I admired the works of the masters in the city's art gallery. I saw Viking treasures in the historical museum and walked the huge columned halls of what was once the royal coach house and which now houses everything from medieval armour and cannon to First World War biplanes, one of Hitler's doodlebugs and modern missiles.

I paid my respects to the wistful mermaid statue – symbol of Copenhagen – and the equally revered bust of Churchill, looking pugnacious, near the touching little Museum of the Resistance – a must for British visitors.

For dinner I again took the advice of the hotel staff and again I was not disappointed. The speciality of the little place they recommended in the Lille Kongensgade was a sort of hotpot so satisfying that it was as well I decided against a starter.

It came sizzling to the table – a cauldron of tender chunks of veal with tomatoes, peas, mushrooms, and onions served with lightly fried potatoes.

For dessert another house favourite – delicious Jutland-style apple cake, dark and rich with brown sugar and blackcurrants and topped with cream. With beer, coffee, and service dinner cost me £10.35. But the atmosphere was beyond price.

A pianist lured diners from their tables to sing and dance. And then, as the red plush and gold Opera House across the road closed, some of the professional singers came into the restaurant, grouped themselves round the piano and took the place over for a programme of carefree songs.

I was up early on Sunday to take a trip for the twenty-mile journey to Rosskilde, a pleasant little town at the head of a misty tree-lined bay with swans gliding among moored cabin cruisers.

I lunched in the museum cafeteria – a huge open sandwich, a slice of marzipan cake, beer and coffee cost me just under £3 and I headed back to Copenhagen.

For dinner I went back to the spot where my visit started – the main railway station. And if that sounds an unromantic, unlikely place for a Sunday dinner abroad I can only tell you that if British Rail could lay on such a spread they would make a fortune.

Beneath the vaulted roof of a columned hall nearly sixty dishes hot and cold, ranging from salmon and shrimps, chicken, beef and hot, spicey specialities to cheeses, fruit and gateaux were arranged on a mighty buffet table to which you could return as often as you liked.

With beer and coffee that dinner cost me just £5.30 and you would have been hard put to it to find a similar bargain anywhere in Europe.

It was in fact yet another bargain of a bargain weekend break. It was a trip that I found, as a British visitor, to be filled with a warmth that even a Scandinavian winter can't dispel. That is the real charm of Copenhagen.

Friday dinner – Peder Oxe.
Friday entertainment – Vin and Olgod.
Saturday lunch – Theatre Cafe.
Saturday dinner – Parnas Bistro.
Sunday lunch – Self-service at Viking Museum, Rosskilde.
Sunday dinner – Buffet at Central Railway Station, Copenhagen.
Hotel – Imperial.

34   A VIKING CRUISE TO GOTHENBURG

On a chilly morning I climbed the gangway to a sleek white ship, joined the throng at the bar, and raised my glass of *akvavit* to a thunderous chorus of '*Skal*' from my fellow passengers.

And in that moment, still well before Harwich had vanished over the misty horizon, I had the distinct feeling that even the cold of a Scandinavian winter was going to be no obstacle to a delightful out-of-season break.

There certainly was no happier way of proving it than by sailing under the Danish flag on the *Tor Britannia* to Sweden. There she was, all 15,000 gleaming tons of her, heading out into the North Sea on this Wednesday midday to reach her cruising speed of twenty-two knots. Ahead lay the 500-mile, twenty-four-hour voyage to Sweden's second city Gothenburg, the first leg of a splendid winter holiday that would last until Sunday evening when she would tie up again at Harwich.

To sail on her, plus two nights at half board in a hotel ashore and a book of vouchers to cut shopping costs in an expensive city, there is a basic package price of just £85.

Tor Britannia is classed as a ferry but the description could not be more misleading.

She has spacious, softly lit bars, a sauna, cinemas, shops selling luxury goods at shipboard prices, a discotheque, a fine restaurant, a lounge with orchestra for dancing and a cafeteria that puts to shame so many establishments bearing the same title on this side of the North Sea.

Her only Spartan aspect is the four-berth cabin you get if you pay the basic fare. For the package is designed for a small group travelling together. If you want a cabin with private shower and toilet you pay supplements according to the number of berths and position on the ship, of £9 to £24.

I lunched in the cafeteria on the advice of some Swedish travellers who suggested that I should save my appetite for dinner.

And the open sandwich, a masterpiece of creamed sea food with mayonnaise, eggs and salad garnish which followed a big bowl of thick vegetable broth, seemed virtually a meal in itself.

With delicious pastries, good coffee and a bottle of beer my lunch cost £3.50.

That evening, in a flower-banked restaurant, I had the choice of a fixed menu or à la carte with waiter service.

But I plumped for the best and most typical Scandinavian of all gastronomic bargains, a *smorgasbord* of over forty hot and cold dishes ranging from marinated salmon and herrings to reindeer steak, ragout, salads, cheeses and marvellous cream gateaux.

With coffee and a half-bottle of wine, dinner cost me £8.50.

In the nightclub, the orchestra – you've got to have a pleasant singing voice as well as being an accomplished musician to entertain in Sweden it seems – switched effortlessly from Swedish to English numbers and back again.

And by next morning, braced by a big buffet breakfast costing £3.30, I was as eager as the Swedes for my first glimpse of Gothenburg.

A coach was waiting to take those of us on the deal to our hotel overlooking the harbour.

Gothenburg provided a welcome as warm as the pavements that they heat on the coldest days. It is a city too where almost everyone seems to speak English.

What a splendid place it is, with the sea god Poseidon on his fountain dominating the great boulevard-like main avenue, modern pedestrian-only shopping arcades, and windows filled with fine pastries and chocolates, gleaming crystal, pewter and silver.

At lunch in a restaurant famed throughout Sweden I tucked into baked halibut with mussels and shrimps in a lobster sauce and served with mixed vegetables.

There were exotic-looking ice creams and concoctions being consumed all around me, but the main course was so rich and satisfying that I contented myself with a plate of little chocolate

and almond cakes served with coffee.

By Swedish standards, the price was reasonable at about £10.40 including beer and service charge.

And it was just the sort of meal to put me in a perfect mood to enjoy Gothenburg. There was so much to admire – the peaceful canalside walks, the Slottsskogen Park with its hills and glades so close to the city centre where reindeer and sea lions seem to be completely at home in surroundings more like a nature reserve.

I enjoyed, too, the pleasure of the city's fine shopping arcades and sampling coffee and Gothenburg's famous chocolate and marzipan cakes.

Back in my hotel on the first night I freshened up for dinner with a sauna, a dip in the heated indoor pool surrounded by palms and flowers and promised myself a suntan in the solarium during my stay.

Then after dinner I could play roulette in the hotel's little casino, dance to records of my choice or relax in the softly lit piano bar.

On Friday night I was more adventurous. I joined a group of fellow British visitors to sample nightlife in the heart of the city.

A stately old building had been transformed into an entertainment centre. There was a pleasant little dance club, a cosy bar, a British-style pub complete with guitarist and open until the early hours, and a big lounge equipped with deep leather armchairs and a crackling open fire where a pianist softly played and sang.

The shipping company also offers a deal allowing you to take your car.

This gives you the freedom to explore the countryside which is close at hand and idyllic – the islands connected by ferries and bridges, the silver-birch and fir forests, the inlets where swans glide, the romantic old-world towns and fishing villages of wooden houses wrapped in winter peace.

But a car is not essential. You can have a fine time as I did without leaving Gothenburg itself.

And when you start your journey home on Saturday evening the welcoming atmosphere on board your ship ensures your Swedish winter holiday is far from over. And even if the North Sea gets choppy you don't seem to care.

For that holiday ends when reluctantly you head down the gangway at Harwich – and not a moment before.

Hotel – Scandinavia.
Thursday lunch – Fiskekrogen.
Thursday dinner – at the hotel.
Friday lunch – Park Avenue Hotel Lunch Club.
Friday dinner – at the hotel.
Entertainment – Gamle Port.

TURKEY

35 ISTANBUL THE EXOTIC

I had seen Istanbul first – by moonlight. I had gazed with fascination from the window of my luxury hotel overlooking the Bosphorus, past silver, slender minarets to the Asian shore.

The narrow waters dividing two continents and the calm expanse of the Sea of Marmara at its mouth had seemed alive with lights – the lights of fussing ferry boats and of cars crossing the great suspension bridge between Europe and Asia, the lamps of the night fishers and of houses on little islands peaceful under it.

Now with the rays of the rising sun slanting into my room and casting a pink glow on the exotic landscape buildings and water before me, I looked out on the scene again to find that my winter-weekend city was as beautiful by day as it had seemed on the night I arrived.

I had come late on Saturday after a four-hour flight from London, to a traditional welcome cocktail in one of my hotel's spacious bars, and a lot of good advice about how to enjoy Istanbul from the courier who had brought visitors like myself by bus from the airport.

And that first look at the city by moonlight had convinced me that I was at the start of a winter break with a difference.

I had chosen the deal they call the Flying Carpet. The basic cost is £236 and for this you have the round trip from London by scheduled service, and five nights' bed and breakfast.

It is, I freely admit, an extravagant piece of self-indulgence.

In addition to the high basic cost you must pay for meals and entertainments in a country where wines and spirits carry a swingeing rate of tax.

Yet at the end of that all-too-brief stay I found myself with only one regret – that I could not have stayed longer. For a winter break in Istanbul is worth all the cost and the long journey. It is unlike any other city on earth. It straddles two continents – it lies on the boundary of the Eastern and the Western worlds.

And classic Istanbul is very beautiful. The domed echoing

The Mosque of Suleiman the Magnificent in Istanbul

magnificence of St Sophia, the glories of the Mosque of Suleiman the Magnificent and of the Blue Mosque, all of which you see on your Saturday-morning city tour included in the deal, are only part of the magic Istanbul has to offer.

When you cross the Galata Bridge over the busy Bosphorus inlet they call the Golden Horn, your excursion bus passes street vendors and fleets of little brightly painted fishing boats and quaysides. Then you return to the cool elegance of your Westernized hotel for lunch.

Even the fine buffet there in a wide-windowed dining room high over the city has more than an Eastern touch. In addition to all the normal hot and cold Western dishes, you can take your pick of Turkish specialities like vine leaves filled with rice, herbs and pine kernels, Caucasian lamb grilled with peppers and served with delicately flavoured rice, and as well as profiteroles there are dishes of sweet honeyed *baklava* and almond cakes.

My Saturday lunch with beer and coffee cost me just under £8 and then I was off to explore the famous covered bazaar where you can bargain for everything from carpets and leatherwork to delicate silver jewellery and long-toed slippers.

I found a fascinating museum, where the winter sun gleams on the spiked helmets and the chain mail of the fierce Turkish warriors who fought the Crusaders.

I walked in the setting sun along the cannon-lined battlements of the castle which the old rulers built to guard the waterways cutting through the city on their course between the sea of Marmara and the Black Sea, and on those battlements I heard the call to prayer from the tops of the minarets.

As the Saturday moon rose over those minarets I climbed the steep stairway to the heights of an old watchtower, now one of Istanbul's leading nightclubs and restaurants.

What a fantastic experience it was. There were whirling folk dancers, the music of pipes and throbbing drums, wild gypsy serenades, dark-eyed bellydancers, weaving sensuously in the dim light of blue and gold lamps, and pretty girls singing ballads.

Dinner was as Turkish as the surroundings – a huge platter of hors d'oeuvres – yoghurt with herbs served in hollowed-out oranges, creamed roes, hot peppers, mussels with piquant fillings, full-flavoured cheeses, and spicey meats.

My main course was Circassian chicken, served in a delicious sauce of creamed chestnuts, garnished with fresh lemon and served with a salad sprinkled with horseradish. My dessert was a feathery-light honey cake. There was thick sweet coffee and a half-bottle of full-bodied Turkish wine.

The cost of my evening out, including the show and the chance to join in general dancing until well into the early hours, was £10.

It was the sort of night out to make you feel like a sultan and for me it was the perfect introduction to the very heart of the world of the sultans on Sunday morning – to the famous Topkapi Palace itself.

The great doors of the harem creaked open and there, among the cool courtyards and pavilions and bath chambers, where the favourites prepared themselves and waited for the summons to their master, I found myself back in past centuries.

In the Treasury building, jewelled thrones and fantastic costumes glittered before me, huge rubies and diamonds flashed, scimitars and gem-encrusted daggers glowed.

I walked through the sultan's rose garden to a kebab-and-sweetmeat lunch in the Palace Restaurant, where I was served by waiters in red, gold and black with brilliant yellow cummerbunds.

Then I boarded a ferry for the fifteen-minute, 30p journey to the Asian side of the Bosphorus.

I walked the colourful narrow streets of the waterfront and climbed Camlica Hill for what was the finest of all views of Istanbul. Little wooden houses were behind me now, the air was sweet with the scent of pinewoods and then before me lay the incredible vista of the Eastern city – its waters, its domes and minarets, castles, palaces and bridges.

I lingered there watching the sun set and the moon rise as thousands must have done before me. Now the city twinkled with lights and it was time to go back down the hill, board my ferry and head for Europe, to a little restaurant beside the water where I had been told that bass baked Turkish-style with mushrooms and tomatoes would be the perfect main course of my last dinner in Istanbul.

I thought as I went that I had never been an enthusiast for that sweet sticky concoction they called Turkish delight.

The real Turkish delight I reflected lay all around me. It was just right for my taste. All its flavour would stay with me long after the domes and minarets of Istanbul had faded over the horizon.

Hotel – Hilton.
Saturday dinner – Galata Tower Nightclub.
Sunday lunch – Topkapi Palace Restaurant.
Sunday dinner – Kalyon Oteli.

ROMANIA

36 LATIN WARMTH BEHIND THE IRON CURTAIN

'*Noroc!*' called the young couple at the next table, raising their brimming glasses of plum brandy to me as they heard a British voice. I lifted my glass to them in response to an age-old Romanian toast and felt a warm glow that wasn't just the result of the fiery stuff I was swallowing.

Through the window of the candlelit restaurant I could see the proud Carpathian peaks of Transylvania soaring against a starry sky high above one of the loveliest valleys of Europe.

I had come in from a night breeze filled with scent of pine and after a perfect Transylvanian day out in the open to dine in local style and to be serenaded with soft gypsy music.

In this Iron Curtain country with a difference I felt I was being made truly welcome – and not for the first time. Unlike their more reserved Slav neighbours, the Romanians are Latins and they have a Latin knack of making the East–West barrier shrink into insignificance. You don't even need to apply for a visa to join them for a holiday.

Now the romantic tempo of the little group of musicians changed – the locals stamped their feet and joined in a song with a beat which had the place ringing.

The food too was splendid. First a dish of charcuterie. My main course was spitted chicken flamed with brandy and served with slices of deliciously tender suckling pig which had rotated slowly over a wood fire.

There was a huge salad of hard-boiled eggs, pickled cucumber and red peppers; there were roast potatoes and hot nutty cakes of country bread. And for dessert, pancakes filled with cream cheese and topped with cream and powdered sugar. And the price for my evening out, including coffee and half a bottle of wine, was just £8.

I was in Poiana Brasov, one of the country's leading mountain resorts – now becoming almost as popular with Western tourists in spring, summer and autumn as it has long been for skiers when the velvet-green slopes sweeping down from the edge of the pine and silver-birch forests are bright with snow instead of glowing with flowers as I saw them.

Each time I see a whirling cloud of swallows under a blue sky I shall remember Poiana Brasov. But those tiny birds will make me think of Bran Castle too. For earlier on in the day when I dined so well to the strains of the gypsy orchestra, I had taken one of Romania's most famous tourist excursions: through gorgeous mountain scenery to the setting of Bram Stoker's novel *Dracula*.

Pinnacled Bran Castle certainly looked the part – towering high on a rock. But swallows and not vampires wheeled around those lofty walls.

As I strolled around rooms filled with armour and hunting trophies and climbed narrow, dimly-lit staircases to view the countryside from the turrets, I learnt that a former owner with the sinister title of Vlad the Impaler had been a sort of model for Dracula. But he was no vampire and he only impaled people who were in favour of the Turks – so the Romanians regard him as a folk hero . . .

If the view from Vlad's walls is impressive, it is nothing compared with the panorama of lakes, mountains and valleys which greet you when you take cable cars to the heights above Poiana Brasov and the older, statelier mountain resort of Sinaia.

And if you can tear yourself away from the roses, and gentians, the rushing trout streams and the heated swimming pools, you can join a reasonably priced day tour to Bucharest, Romania's capital city where a replica of the Arc de Triomphe and radiating wide boulevards give more than a touch of Paris.

But the mountains are only part of the Romanian tourist

Bran Castle . . . fictional home of Dracula

scene. To the east, beyond the plains and huge wheatfields, lie the warm, calm waters of the Black Sea and a coastline which stretches nearly 200 miles from the Russian border in the north to Bulgaria in the south.

The beaches are wide and smooth, the temperature in high summer often gets into the nineties, the sun shines for twelve hours a day.

To my mind the best way to enjoy Romania is to divide your holiday between mountains and coast. From Mamaia, the besk-known resort near the old city of Constantza, the holiday coast runs south.

Eforie and Neptun are particularly attractive, but for me Mamaia stands supreme. On one side of the town, the Black Sea stretches away into the sun-haze; on the other, a wide, fresh lake ideal for sailing, water-skiing, windsurfing, fishing for carp, roach and bream.

Both mountains and sea resorts offer nightlife. In Neptun, for instance, you can dine off Romanian specialities, see a local-style show and dance until the early hours for about £10.

Romania, like most European countries, is geared principally to package tours with air fare included and there is a big range available. Reckon on about £270 for two weeks with full board and split between the mountains and the Black Sea.

To see more of the country itself you can take a fly-drive package from £260 for a stay-put week by the sea with full board, and seven days' touring, hotels included, in a car with unlimited mileage.

If you prefer to take your own car you can buy a £125 package for eleven nights, first-class hotel accommodation with half board.

But independent travellers are welcome too. You can find comfortable hotels charging about £15 a day half board and camp sites where a family of four with a car and caravan pay around £3 a day in fees. And Romania is well worth the effort of driving there.

To me there was something highly satisfying about making a short trip from modern Mamaia to Constantza where the centuries seem to roll away and you climb the minaret of the Turkish mosque to look out over the roofs of the old city.

Just as satisfying, in fact, as finding so close to my up-to-date hotel in Sinaia a beautiful old monastery where grave, bearded monks show you their silver icons and other treasures while swallows circle overhead in the warm air.

For sheer delight I recommend an admittedly pricey extra. For a package rate of £30 I was driven by coach to a town on the

Danube a few miles from Mamaia. And there I boarded a century-old stern-wheeled paddle steamer for a day's cruise steaming slowly among the reed beds, the pelicans, the fishermen's thatched cottages on the romantic delta which stretches to the Russian border.

You stop for lunch with wine – creamy fish soup, juicy carp and those special Romanian pancakes. And somehow that day in such a beautiful timeless place just doesn't seem long enough.

Then you come back to the lights of Mamaia twinkling under the moon. You are more than ready for a glass of plum brandy to whet your dinner appetite. And in just the mood to raise it and toast the newcomers as the locals toasted you when you first arrived.

'*Noroc!*'

Dinner at Mamaia – International Hotel.
Lunch on Danube Delta – restaurant used by excursion ship (changes all the time).
Meal at Poiana Brasov – Coliba Haiducilor.

SPAIN

37 THE BIZARRE BEAUTY OF LANZAROTE

What a glorious Lanzarote day – my first on a Spanish Canary Island fascinatingly different from all the others.

It began with breakfast beside my villa pool set in a garden bright with oleander, bougainvillaea and hibiscus and with a view beyond olive groves and dazzling white houses to the Atlantic at its calmest.

I was at Puerto del Carmen, the island's main tourist centre on the south coast where the superb golden beaches are a swimmer's paradise for nine months out of twelve. But when I headed inland in a hired car to explore Lanzarote, the contrasts I found were fantastic.

There to the north-west was the Atlantic again. But now it creamed and roared far below a mighty rock arch spanning rearing cliffs.

And the landscape of Arab-type houses set among palm trees and windmills changed before my eyes into mountainous scenery so uncannily like the surface of the moon that it was almost impossible to believe I was still on our planet, let alone a small Atlantic island . . .

They call them the Fire Mountains and the Mountains of the Moon, these spectacular heights which soar in the sombre shades – black, dark green and brownish-red – of lava deposits left from volcanic eruptions of centuries past. To climb one mighty slope of loose shifting ash I had to abandon the car and mount a camel, the island's main beast of burden. It was worth the long swaying journey to the top – the view from the summit of mountains and craters made me feel even further removed from Earth.

I lunched deep in that weird landscape, watching through the wide windows of a restaurant, where they cook by volcanic heat, as the locals climbed the rocks to grill their fish, chops, sausages and eggs in the natural ovens created by the one volcano which still shows signs of life.

My meal began with tiny new potatoes cooked in their skins and rubbed with rough salt and served with goats' cheese in a deliciously piquant sauce of herbs and spices. The main course was lamb, cooked on a volcanic grill and brought with mixed vegetables. And for dessert I had splendid little full-flavoured Canary bananas flamed in orange juice, banana liqueur, and brandy.

That lunch in a marvellous setting, and including coffee and a half-bottle of Lanzarote wine, cost me just £6. And like virtually every other delight awaiting me on Lanzarote, it was great value.

Then it was back to the other world of Lanzarote for the afternoon – to swim and sunbathe on the south coast. Later I watched a superb sunset over the mountains and joined my friends who had invited me to share their rented villa for a few days, for dinner in a candlelit Puerto del Carmen restaurant specializing in refreshing *gazpacho* followed by sea bream baked in onions and tomatoes and served with chilli and cayenne sauce – fabulous.

But then 'fabulous' exactly describes a Lanzarote holiday. The island – about forty miles from north to south and fourteen from east to west – offers so much. There are delightful beaches, warmed by twelve hours' sunshine a day with the thermometer heading into the nineties in high summer and hardly ever going below the sixties in mid-winter.

You can sail and windsurf, fish for everything from mullet and mackerel to barracuda and tuna and dive for octopus and crab. You can play golf and tennis, hire a horse, take boat trips to idyllic islands like Graciosa and Fuerteventura.

There are romantic old white-walled towns like Teguise and Yaiza to explore and the oasis-like Valley of the Thousand Palms is a pleasure to the eye. There are battlements to climb, still bristling with the old cannon which defended the island against Corsairs; and cool caverns of cathedral-like beauty.

And there is that incredible landscape. Away from the Fire Mountains generations of islanders have cultivated the rich soil beneath a covering of black volcanic ash to grow grapes and melons, figs and some of the best tomatoes and onions you'll eat anywhere.

It seldom rains on Lanzarote, but the ash acts as a perfect filter for the heavy dew. So the residue of the old eruptions has been turned to the best possible use.

Lanzarote is geared to package tours – travelling independently is long and expensive; there is no direct scheduled air or sea service from Britain. And the accent is on self-catering. A package this summer including flight and a fortnight's stay in a three-bedroomed villa like the one my friends chose costs from £300 per head. For slightly cheaper prices you can rent an apartment or bungalow. If you prefer to stay in an hotel for two weeks' half board, reckon on an average price of about £400.

On a self-catering deal a family of four can cope comfortably on just over £40 a week for food shopping. A bottle of reasonable wine costs as little as 50p. And as Lanzarote is a free port you can buy twenty British cigarettes for 30p and a litre of Scotch for £5. To hire a car costs about £50 a week with unlimited mileage.

On my last Lanzarote day I lunched in the sun-filled courtyard of a rambling country house – now a restaurant – at the foot of a monument erected as a tribute to the islanders who had made their little stricken domain so fertile.

Looking at that monument as we sat lazing in the sunshine after our meal, we all had the same idea – why was it necessary to build it? The tough farmers of old who had triumphed over appalling adversity to make their island flourish had left the best of all monuments for the rest of us to enjoy: Lanzarote itself.

Volcanic meal – El Diable.
Seaside meal – Cangrejo Rojo.
Meal near monument – El Monumento.

38 HOW TO SEE ANDALUSIA WITHOUT CROWDS

It was the moment I had waited for, the moment when the Alhambra – its Moorish battlements and towers gleaming pink and backed by the mighty peaks of the Sierra Nevada – came dramatically into view around a curve of my road to the city of Granada.

And gazing at the magnificence of the setting, at the dark green of the cypress groves and the gently waving palms and already catching the scent of the blooms in its gardens, I remembered the words of the Spaniard I had met on the plane to Seville.

When I told him I was touring Andalusia on a week's off-season fly-drive package deal, he said quietly: 'Senhor, you will see much beauty as you travel but Granada is special, believe me.'

I drove on into the city past the statue of Columbus showing the plans of his voyage to the New World to his patron, the Queen of Spain.

And soon I was behind the towering walls of the Alhambra where in 1492, the year Columbus made his famous discovery across the Atlantic, the same Queen's forces ended seven centuries of Moorish occupation of southern Spain and hoisted over the Alhambra the identical red and gold flag I was to see in Granada's treasure house.

I steeped myself in the beauty of a long-gone world preserved by Spain with loving care. Here in the last Moorish fastness in all Europe I found courtyards shaded by orange trees and bright with bougainvillaea and jasmine. Only the tinkle of fountains broke the stillness.

Ceilings were bright with multi-coloured tiles and there were elaborately carved, decorated walls.

I looked out at a Moorish king's view of his own city – the white houses with terracotta roofs rising up the mountainside and the old battlements stretching into the sun haze and snaking up the slopes.

And on the hill next to the Alhambra I found even lovelier gardens where flowers bloom all the year round, where the

Moors had harnessed the waters cascading from the mountains to form dozens of fountains splashing into pools bright with lilies.

The Spaniard on the Seville plane had not over-painted his picture of Granada.

I thought, too, that the day trips taken by so many British

tourists staying on the Costa del Sol could never be long enough to absorb the atmosphere of it all. They would certainly not see this lovely place as I did, when the moon rose over the Alhambra.

And when, in the most enchanting moments of a two-and-a-half-hour show in a city famed throughout Spain for its flamenco and classical dancing, five dark-eyed girls in red dresses with black *mantillas* clicked castanets and danced to the lyrical melody of 'Granada'.

But seeing it all without hassle is one of the joys of the deal I had chosen. For two of the seven nights you spend in Spain are reserved for Granada.

There may be less pricey ways of passing an out-of-season week but I can think of none more rewarding than this Spanish holiday with a difference, the happiest of all proofs that the land which draws more British tourists than any other, has so much more to offer than the sands and the modern hotels of the Costa del Sol and Majorca.

Depending on the date that you travel, you pay from £197 to £217 and the top price does not include a hefty surcharge for Christmas and the last days of March.

You have an eight-day holiday, flying to and from Seville, the capital city of Andalusia, by scheduled flight, a self-drive car with unlimited mileage, and three nights in Seville, two in Cordoba, and two in Granada, staying in three-star hotels complete with private bath, plus breakfast and one lunch or dinner per day.

The hotels provide a fair standard of international *cuisine*. But because you are on a half-board deal, it is easy to eat in real Spanish style and atmosphere by choosing an outside restaurant for lunch or dinner.

And in all of the three cities, and on your drives through the plains, the orange and olive groves and the rolling foothills, there is fine value for your pesetas.

In the shadow of the Alhambra, for instance, you can eat at a multi-dish buffet with wine for £5 and be serenaded by guitars.

I had spent my first night in Seville and it was not nearly long enough to explore that lovely old city, but enough to give me a foretaste of what I would enjoy when I returned by a different route for the last two days of my trip.

You enter Cordoba over a bridge which has spanned the River Guadalquivir since half a century before Christ.

What a gorgeous city this is with its palaces and its fountains, its Street of Flowers lined by dazzling white houses with balconies filled with blooms, its shops selling filigree jewellery, and its superb local leather works.

Imagine too walking into an ancient mosque through pink and white Eastern arches and columns and then suddenly hearing the sound of the Mass echoing through the stillness. For in the heart of the mosque is one of Spain's most magnificent cathedrals.

I lunched in an elegant restaurant. First, an aperitif of the sherry type of a local wine called montilla. The *gazpacho* was perfect.

And the classic seafood meat and rice dish paella came sizzling to the table in its pan. The main course was tender charcoal-grilled beef in a subtle sauce. And from a laden sweet trolley, I chose the house speciality, glacé pumpkin, in a feathery-light pastry. I had a third of a litre jug of *sangria* and ended with good coffee.

And the price for all of this was an astonishing £5.

In Seville I saw the most touching of all Andalusian statues – the figure of a boy clinging to the masthead and pointing excitedly forward.

A local lad was the first to spot the New World after an epic voyage which began when Columbus sailed down Seville's river towards the open sea.

I loved the streets lined with orange trees, the sunlit squares where fountains splash away the centuries.

I came home with so many memories of Granada, of the castles and the sleepy villages, of sunlit plains and the olive groves, of the distant views of mountains, where the peaks will be whitened soon by the only snow you'll see on your Andalusian holiday.

But back under grey British October skies I recall vividly my last night in Seville.

Spain's largest cathedral looked magnificent under the soft floodlighting as did the fountains and the great curving palace of the Captain-General of Andalusia – what romantic titles the Spanish give their dignitaries.

Dinner in a candlelit restaurant was superb. There was hot soup, rich in herbs and spices, meat and vegetables.

My main course was a succulent bass flammed in spirits, cooked with fennel, served with cauliflower and mushrooms and accompanied by a sauce of creamed shrimps and crayfish, grapes and almonds.

The dessert was fine, too: the lightest of puddings topped with ice cream, whipped cream and caramel.

And the price with coffee and half a bottle of wine was a little over £9.

Then came the last flamenco show of my trip. It cost me just over £5 for admission, and one drink.

And to end my evening, while tingling guitar music was still running through my head, I had a gentle ride in a horsedrawn carriage back to my hotel past moon-gilded palms and banks of oleander.

For me it was the perfect round-off to a week of old world Spanish magic.

Hotels – Seville: Don Paco.
Cordoba: Los Gallos.
Granada: Los Angeles.
Lunch at Carmona – The Paradon.
Lunch at Cordoba – El Caballo Rojo.
Dinner at Seville – Los Alcazares.
Flamenco show at Granada – Jardines Neptuno.
Buffet lunch at Granada – Bolinario.

BELGIUM

39   THE SPELL
OF THE ARDENNES

From my perch high on the ramparts of Dinant's citadel, I watched spring come to the Ardennes – and a lovely sight it was. The rainclouds which had dogged me on the motorway from the Channel coast all morning seemed to blow away in the breeze from the pine-clad hills, the sun broke through and set the jumbled wet roofs of the town far below me sparkling like diamonds.

Everything seemed to come to life; the waters of the Meuse winding between dramatic cliffs began to gleam and passing little launches edged from the shore with the first tourists of the season bound for one of the most rewarding river trips you can make anywhere in Europe.

I watched those launches as, toy-like from my height, they swung around the bends of the river heading for Namur past castles and towering headlands.

And as the sun grew warmer on my face, it did not take much imagination to see the waters of the Meuse as they will be in the coming weeks – complete with darting canoes and bright with sails.

Now it was time to take the cable car down the cliff face, past Dinant's famous onion-domed church to walk along cobbled, narrow streets past shops with windows full of Europe's most delicious gingerbread, cream cakes and praline chocolates.

Time to drive further into the heart of a delightful Belgian holiday region of huge forests, rolling hills, pinnacled châteaux, lakes, rushing rivers, waterfalls and idyllic villages stretching to Holland in the north, Germany and Luxembourg in the east and France in the south-west.

This is the real Belgium, a hundred times more fascinating than the flat green meadows you meet when you drive east along the mororway from the Channel ferry.

It is off that motorway, as you leave so many thousands of British families to more familiar and distant holiday destinations, that the charm of the Ardennes captures you.

Choose the Ardennes – so easy to reach from Britain – and you choose a natural holiday region which offers everything from swimming, sailing, windsurfing, water-skiing and shooting rapids in a canoe to trout and pike fishing, rock climbing, golf, tennis and riding.

It has fascinating castles and grottoes to explore. It is dotted with some of the most romantic old towns you can find anywhere on the Continent. And you can get marvellous views from the lofty ramparts of Namur, the city which stands at the edge of the Ardennes.

The region's food is simply fabulous. I remember with affection the large trout with cream and almonds, the game in rich wine sauces, the feathery-light apple puddings, rich with cinnamon and brandy and the delicious fruit flans.

The *cuisine* is basically French, but with some special Ardennes touches which made even the most discriminating French visitor smack his lips.

For my first meal there I chose one of the most attractive little towns in the region – La Roche. Its setting beside a fast-flowing river and in a wooded valley is even more dramatic than Dinant's. Its pastries are even more famous and deservedly so.

In an unpretentious little restaurant there I was served full-flavoured leek broth, then tiny cheesecakes with a touch of nutmeg, and the superb Ardennes ham; then wild boar in cream and red wine with cranberries and croquet potatoes. And for dessert there was a fine blueberry flan.

With coffee and a quarter-litre of Luxembourg wine, my lunch cost me £9.50 – and you are not likely to pay less for a four-course good full meal in Belgium. But you can eat much less elaborately than I did in La Roche, and still thoroughly enjoy the experience.

One of my happiest memories was of sitting among the chestnut trees beside a waterfall at Han and eating a huge omelette made with that fine Ardennes ham and accompanied by rough country bread and a big block of creamy butter – no wretched little plastic packets in that establishment. Following the omelette came a generous slice of my hostess's home-made coffee gateau. With a beer I paid £5.50 for my simple but delicious lunch.

And it was made even more pleasant for me by the fact that from the little restaurant I could watch early visitors to Han's famous undercliff grotto emerging in boats – as I had done earlier that day – blinking in the strong sunshine and obviously feeling that nothing underground was quite so appealing to the eye as the blue sky awaiting them at the end of their trip.

In fact, it is the more simple pleasures which make an Ardennes holiday so satisfying.

At Maredsous Abbey the monks serve visitors with home-made bread, cheese and tankards of foaming beer. Bread, cheese and a tankard costs you about 90p.

The Ardennes region is geared mainly to holidays with a car. And if you yearn for solitude you can find miles of forest with only the occasional flitting deer for company. Anywhere more romantic for a quiet picnic would be hard to find, even in the height of summer.

It is easy enough to have a pricey evening out – a few main centres and casinos and some nightlife. But it is easier still to find a comfortable little cafe where you can relax over a good Belgian beer for about 40p after a day under a sun which might not roast you in Mediterranean style, but can often be warm enough to give you a tan.

Where to stay? Dinant and La Roche are ideal choices. There's the attractive wooded area they call Trois Frontières where you can stroll into Germany and Holland on a country walk. I also liked St Hubert with its rustling forests and little Bouillon where the castle is fascinating to see.

Spa has an old-world charm. In Huy the perfume of the

blooms they sell in the market square seems to follow you as you climb the heights above the town for a fine view. There's little Durbuy snug in a pretty valley and sleepy Celles.

And the cost? There are small family hotels and pensions charing £10 a day for half board and £7 for bed and breakfast, and many places offer reductions to young children sharing parents' rooms.

For campers there are well-equipped sites costing around £4 a day for a family of four. Allow about £75 a week for shopping for four people.

If you prefer a package holiday but taking your own car, there's a £60 deal for each of four people including ferry fares and a week in a bungalow – you can also stay for two weeks from roughly £86.

But however you travel and wherever you stay in the Ardennes, I guarantee you will leave with a score of memories. One that stands out in my mind is of an amazed young couple – obviously honeymooners – near Celles.

Beside the road, rusting, ugly and squat, stood a German Tiger tank. It marked the spot where on a snowy Christmas Eve in 1944 Hitler's last desperate gamble – the Ardennes offensive – reached its limit.

They were staring at it as though that tank was something dropped into that lovely setting from outer space: it had no business there. Then they looked at one another, shrugged, smiled and drove on. And I could swear that the birds in the woods nearby sang all the sweeter as they went.

I hope those two were just starting their Ardennes stay – I cannot think of a happier way of putting unpleasantness behind you.

Meal in La Roche – Restaurant Ardennais.
Meal at Han – Le Pavillon.

GIBRALTAR

40 THE WELCOMING ROCK

'We're in luck today, folks – our beauties are all here.' Mike Lawrence – Dolphin Mike to the people of Gibraltar – sang out the words above the throb of *Sea Marauder*'s engine. He pointed ahead of the bows of his sleek catamaran to a group of dorsal fins breaking the surface. Seconds later the dolphins came swarming around us, gleaming black and grey, chasing each other over and through our power wave, standing on their tails for a brief instant, rolling joyfully with ease and grace . . . close enough for us to touch.

'You can stroke 'em, lady,' Mike told one hesitant passenger. 'They love it – this isn't a scene from *Jaws*.' We reached out to them as they gambolled close to the boat's sides and we stroked those wild dolphins far out there in the bay just as though they were domestic pets.

'They know the boat,' Mike explained. 'When they're not busy feeding they always come. They're my dozen regulars – I can always tell them apart from the ones on the Dolphin Highway through the Straits from the West Indies to the Aegean.'

For a small group of British visitors spending a few out-of-season days beneath the blue skies of Gibraltar it was an exhilarating two-and-a-half-hour trip for just £8 a head. You couldn't help sharing Mike's enthusiasm for his dolphins. And you marvelled how he managed, single-handed, to cope with telling us about them, dispensing drinks, controlling the boat – and giving his own racy colourful commentary on the history of the mighty limestone Rock itself.

If dolphins are Mike Lawrence's passion, Gibraltar is his hobby. And it struck me that even if we had not been lucky enough to see the dolphins there were so many other sights to fascinate us that day. There can be few places on earth more majestically beautiful as the setting Mike showed us: the Rock rearing 1,400 feet, the mountains of Andalusia and the white houses of Algeciras across the bay. And on the far side of the straits which divide the Atlantic and the Mediterranean, the towering peaks on the African shore dominated by the Moroccan mountain the ancients called one of the Pillars of Hercules – Gibraltar itself is the other.

Reluctantly we left the dolphins to their frolics and headed back to the Rock. For all his knowledge of its stormy past of

sieges and heroism, Mike Lawrence would be the first to tell you there is no more misleading description of the Rock today than Fortress Gibraltar with the implication in the title of it being just a glorified defence point.

This passionately loyal British territory of just two and three quarter square miles where everyone speaks English and sterling is the currency, has an enchantment all its own. Go there for a winter or early-spring break and you would be unlucky if the thermometer was not touching the sixties. Bougainvillaea, oleander, jacaranda, hibiscus and wisteria give it colour, eucalyptus and palms seem to soften the severe outline of the Rock itself.

You won't sizzle there, but it is easy to get a tan and often the sea is warm enough for a dip from a wide beach, all the more pleasant for being empty of the crowds of high-summer season.

Gibraltar town is a little busier than it was before the Spaniards recently opened their border gates, closed in 1969 as part of their campaign to wrest Gibraltar back from us. Today while Gibraltarians are free to walk across the border to buy fruit and vegetables in the market at La Linea or to bask on the beaches of the Costa del Sol, Spaniards are equally free to stroll into Gibraltar and join visitors from Britain to shop in Main Street, famous for low-taxed perfume, jewellery, curios and other luxury goods. There 200 British cigarettes cost £5 and a bottle of Scotch £3.

The frontier – just yards from the jetty airstrip where you land at the end of your flight from London – is still closed to tourists from the United Kingdom, but you can have a delightful few days in Gib without feeling either claustrophobic or bored.

Apart from its magnificent setting there's the sheer romance of the place, rich in history. You see the spot where they brought Nelson's body ashore from the battered *Victory* after Trafalgar, the touching little cemetery where his dead sailors lie. Climb to the Moorish Tower of Homage, which has stood since centuries before our Norman Conquest and you find yourself almost ready to duck at the sight of an uncannily realistic figure of a hawk-faced turbaned archer, aiming at you from the battlements. Above him flies the biggest of all Gib's vast collection of Union Jacks. The locals fly it day and night; they are determined to keep it there for ever.

There are the galleries dug out of the rock and lined with bristling cannon once manned by British garrisons withstanding sieges of long ago, the lovely gardens filled with subtropical plants and trees. There is St Michael's Cave, of cathedral-like splendour and fabulous acoustics where, if you are lucky enough to hear a symphony concert or military band, see a ballet or an opera, a display of flamenco dancing or even listen to a pop recital, you will emerge wondering just what your ears and eyes have been missing for so many years . . .

You'll take the little red cable car to the heights of the Rock, past the domain of the famous Gibraltar apes and the peaceful sunlit slopes coated with narcissus, blooming cactus, fig, pine and fir trees and olive groves. You are overwhelmed by the incredible view of toy-like ships plying the straits and the glorious arc of the Costa del Sol beaches vanishing into the distant haze. And if you can take your eyes from that panorama you'll find that a simple picnic tastes like a rare feast in the clean air.

Add to all this the pleasures of windsurfing, of fishing from the shore for mackerel, bream and bass, joining expeditions for grouper and skate and diving for octopus and crab and later relaxing in your horsedrawn carriage while police with British-type helmets control the traffic, and you will come to the conclusion, as I did, that Gibraltar is a grand little spot to visit.

A number of tour operators arrange winter and early spring breaks there. The deal I chose cost an average of £140, the price varying with the time of travel. It gives you the round flight from Britain and seven nights in a comfortable hotel on the shores of Caleta Bay, complete with buffet breakfast and room with private bath. You are entertained with accordion, guitar and piano serenades and there is a pleasant little disco.

Gibraltar, as famous for its wealth of national *cuisines*, both Eastern and Western, as for its colourful shopping, is the ideal spot for eating out. Yards from the hotel I dined one night with two fellow visitors in a cheerful, noisy, unpretentious little place where three courses with wine and coffee and including a sizzling main dish of that Spanish meat, chicken, seafood and rice masterpiece, paella, cost us a total of £20. And on another evening I dined in more style at a restaurant in Irish Town where for £10, including a half-bottle of wine, I enjoyed eggs northern-Spanish-style poached with tomatoes, sweet pepper and ham; tender swordfish steak with onions, parsley, paprika and wine; and for dessert a fine fruit-topped cheesecake.

Hotel food is largely international, but as the best of all reminders that lies within sight of the Moroccan shore, the hotel I chose offers a real Moorish feast in rich Eastern setting for just £7.50.

Relaxing in the speciality restaurant with its ornate lamps and decorated Moorish arches, I was served a spicy meat and vegetable broth called *chorbat*; then *couscous*, tender lamb with nuts, fruit, spices and mixed vegetables on a bed of silky semolina; orange salad sprinkled with cinnamon, and to end I had refreshing mint tea and delicious little almond sweetmeats.

If an evening like that puts you in the mood to sample the genuine Moorish atmosphere you'll take as I did a £33 day trip to North Africa – a twenty-minute flight to the minarets, casbah, snake charmers, veiled women and colourful bazaars of Tangier.

You'll drive past the umbrella pine and through green rolling hills to Cape Spartel, the north-west tip of Africa, where camels wait to take you on a swaying ride, where miles of beaches gleam and you are deafened by the Atlantic breakers crashing into the Caves of Hercules.

You lunch exotically in Tangier with sensuous bellydancers and lithe jugglers to entertain you and later you fly back to that tiny piece of Britain perched on the edge of Europe and suddenly feel you are home again.

Even the pubs are British-style, but no pub in Britain stays open from early morning to well past midnight . . . There's a plush casino if you feel extravagant, little dance clubs open until the early hours. And the promise of another beautiful day when the sun rises again.

Perhaps that will be your last full day in Gib. Perhaps like me you'll want to spend part of it high on the Rock looking out on that glorious view of the meeting place of two worlds, two continents and two seas. One thousand four hundred feet below you a plane is taking off for winter chill. You watch it wheel away and hate the idea that your holiday is nearly over.

But tonight there will be another splendid sunset, the sea will be alive with the bobbing lamps of the fishing boats and you cheer up with the thought that Gibraltar is still yours for another twenty-four enchanted hours.

Fish meal at Irish Town – El Patio.
Meal near hotel – Mermaid.

Appendix
NATIONAL TOURIST OFFICES

BELGIUM: Belgian National Tourist Office, 38 Dover Street, London W1. Tel: 499 5379

CYPRUS: Cyprus Tourist Office, 213 Regent Street, London W1. Tel: 734 9822

DENMARK: Danish Tourist Office, 169–173 Regent Street, London W1. Tel: 734 2637

FRANCE: French Government Tourist Office, 178 Piccadilly, London W1. Tel: 499 6911

GIBRALTAR: Gibraltar Tourist Office, Arundel Great Court, 179 The Strand, London WC2. Tel: 836 0777

GREECE: National Tourist Organization of Greece, 195–197 Regent Street, London W1. Tel: 734 5997

HOLLAND: Dutch Tourist Office, 143 New Bond Street, London W1. Tel: 499 9367

ITALY: Italian State Tourist Office, 1 Princes Street, London W1. Tel: 408 1254

NORWAY: Norwegian National Tourist Office, 20 Pall Mall, London SW1. Tel: 839 6255

PORTUGAL: Portuguese Tourist Office, New Bond Street House, 1–5 New Bond Street, London W1. Tel: 493 3873

ROMANIA: Romanian Tourist Office, 77–81 Gloucester Place, London W1. Tel: 935 8590

SPAIN: Spanish Tourist Office, 57/58 St James's Street, London SW1. Tel: 499 0901

SWEDEN: Swedish Tourist Office, 3 Cork Street, London W1. Tel: 437 5816

SWITZERLAND: Swiss National Tourist Office, 1 New Coventry Street, London W1. Tel: 734 1921

TURKEY: Turkish Tourism Information Office, 170 Piccadilly London W1. Tel: 734 8681